Gerhart Hauptmann's *Before Daybreak*

UNC | COLLEGE OF ARTS AND SCIENCES
Germanic and Slavic Languages and Literatures

From 1949 to 2004, UNC Press and the UNC Department of Germanic & Slavic Languages and Literatures published the UNC Studies in the Germanic Languages and Literatures series. Monographs, anthologies, and critical editions in the series covered an array of topics including medieval and modern literature, theater, linguistics, philology, onomastics, and the history of ideas. Through the generous support of the National Endowment for the Humanities and the Andrew W. Mellon Foundation, books in the series have been reissued in new paperback and open access digital editions. For a complete list of books visit www.uncpress.org.

Gerhart Hauptmann's
Before Daybreak
A Translation and an Introduction

PETER BAULAND

UNC Studies in the Germanic Languages and Literatures
Number 92

Copyright © 1978

This work is licensed under a Creative Commons CC BY-NC-ND license. To view a copy of the license, visit http://creativecommons.org/licenses.

Suggested citation: Bauland, Peter. *Gerhart Hauptmann's Before Daybreak: A Translation and an Introduction*. Chapel Hill: University of North Carolina Press, 1978. DOI: https://doi.org/10.5149/9781469657547_Hauptmann

Library of Congress Cataloging-in-Publication Data
Names: Bauland, Peter.
Title: Gerhart Hauptmann's Before Daybreak : A translation and an introduction / by Peter Bauland.
Other titles: University of North Carolina Studies in the Germanic Languages and Literatures ; no. 92.
Description: Chapel Hill : University of North Carolina Press, [1978] Series: University of North Carolina Studies in the Germanic Languages and Literatures. | Includes bibliographical references.
Identifiers: LCCN 78007210 | ISBN 978-1-4696-2994-0 (pbk: alk. paper) | ISBN 978-1-4696-5754-7 (ebook)
Classification: LCC PT2616 .V6 E5 1978 | DCC 832/ .8

For ABBY

*who is patient and loving—
and who, unlike me, came by her German the hard way*

Contents

Acknowledgments	x
Introduction	xi
On Translating *Vor Sonnenaufgang*	xxi
A Note on the Text	xxiv

Before Daybreak

Floorplans of the First Edition	3
Dramatis Personae	4
Act I	5
Act II	28
Act III	41
Act IV	57
Act V	69
Select Bibliography	85

Acknowledgments

I am grateful to the Horace H. Rackham School of Graduate Studies of the University of Michigan whose kind support has made the publication of *Before Daybreak* possible.

The translation of Gerhart Hauptmann's *Vor Sonnenaufgang* is from the original text as it appears in *Sämtliche Werke*, Band I: *Dramen*. Centenar-Ausgabe, ©1966 Verlag Ullstein GmbH (Propyläen Verlag), Frankfurt/M-Berlin, and appears here with the publisher's kind permission.

Ann Arbor, Michigan   Peter Bauland
October 1977

Introduction

The premiere of *Vor Sonnenaufgang* in 1889 was what the Germans like to refer to hyperbolically as a *Theaterskandal*, the kind of play that arouses not only controversy among critics but also violent responses (and sometimes less than polite action) in the ranks of the theatergoing public. Ever since Schiller had declared that the drama was a moral institution, an intellectual and spiritual arena in which a people's ideas and ethics are debated in living, dramatic form, a substantial portion of Germany's audience has taken its playgoing very seriously. Met with both outrage and admiration, *Vor Sonnenaufgang* was the first important play of the German Naturalist movement; it was also the first play by Gerhart Hauptmann, the most significant Naturalist of the theater.

"Naturalism" is a term too frequently used interchangeably with "Realism." They are not mutually exclusive concepts, but there is an essential difference between the two. Realism is primarily an artistic technique; Naturalism is predominantly a view of the human condition. The Realist in the theater will try to create the stage illusion of life and language as we all know them from common experience. At his most extreme, he will attempt to re-create the documentary truth by means of the most blatant theatrical lie: that what we are watching is actual life, not an interpretation of it on a stage. Those who denigrate this form of drama as craftless or dishonest would do well to remember Picasso's definition of all art as a magnificent species of lies that forces us to see the truth. The Naturalist follows the teachings of the great mid-nineteenth-century scientists (Darwin, Lyell, et al.) and the dicta that Zola, the Goncourts, and their disciples derived from them with the help of the major English, French, and German philosophers and historians of that era. Although most Naturalists believed that vigorous and concentrated human effort could ameliorate grim social conditions, they nevertheless maintained that in a capricious and possibly meaningless universe, man has little power over his own destiny, for his fate is determined by forces essentially outside his control. Neither his moral choices nor even the meeting of volition and circumstance gives man any arsenal with which to combat the indomitable natural and social forces of heredity and environment. The milieu makes the man; this is the law of nature.

While the Naturalists had established a modicum of respectability for themselves in fiction, the theater was still largely the domain of the genteel and the affluent, who were intolerant of unmannerly intrusions on their entertainment even in Germany, which was more receptive to the experiments of the "new theater" than were the other countries of Western Europe. In Berlin, particularly in the theater of Otto Brahm's Freie Bühne, Ibsen's plays had found a stage in the 1880s; but dramatists who dwelled on matters more brutal and sordid than those delineated in the work of the Norwegian giant had difficulty finding professional theaters hospitable to their plays. And Ibsen, after all, is actually tangential to the mainstream of hard-line Naturalism. His plays are frequently cited, particularly in the English-speaking world, as illustrative of the movement, but this may well be an act of desperation occasioned by the lack of available English texts of works closer to the center of Naturalism, which usually tend to be more provincial and dialect-ridden than Ibsen's. Antoine's Théâtre Libre in Paris was founded in 1887, but it was essentially an amateur company. Grein's theater in London, the Abbey Players, Strindberg's Intimate Theater in Stockholm, the Moscow Art Theater—all these had yet to be established when Brahm's theater in Berlin became, in 1889, the only first-rate house in Europe that dared to perform Naturalistic drama.

Brahm and his associates felt it their responsibility to stage what they conceived to be a faithful reproduction of reality, but from the very beginning, it was the scurvier aspects of reality upon which both managers and playwrights concentrated. The Naturalists' "slice of life" seemed always to be cut from the bottom. A throughly, even if justifiably pessimistic lot, they sought the evidence to support their stance, let the part stand for the whole, and said, "This is the truth," which would have been a statement no less cogent or powerful had it been, "This is one of the horrible parts of the truth." The insistent and unrelieved *Elendsmalerei* ("depiction of total misery") ultimately undermined Naturalism's courageous and socially, as well as artistically, influential dramatization of human suffering. At its best, Naturalistic drama had a human and social vision that far transcended mere journalistic verisimilitude; at its worst, it was conventional melodrama that demonstrated only the surface details of the lives of the wretched. The finest plays of Naturalism had power, imagination, and dignity as well as social awareness. They were exceedingly moving, and they underscored the sordid by soaring above it. Beneath their surface statement of the limitations of human flesh was often an irrepressible belief in the capabilities of the human spirit.

German Naturalism, more so than any other, was politically and socioeconomically oriented. It had a strong proletarian bent, and many of its practitioners had at least a passing connection with socialism, though it would be hard to find any two of them with identical views. The Germans particularly eschewed the tradition of the dramatic hero and espoused instead the everyday heroism of groups of people doing their futile best to hack their way through life. Nevertheless, the subject matter of Naturalistic plays was much the same in Germany as elsewhere: small-town life among farmers, miners, and tradesmen; the big-city working class under expanding industrialization; the evils of class systems and the destructive conflicts they engendered; the hollow conventions of middle-class society where respectability posed as morality. The drama of Naturalism frequently concentrated upon disease, alcoholism, illegitimacy, and the problems of adolescence and education. Social reform and those who fight for it were often the central dramatic strain. Throughout Naturalism's canon, we find the incompatibility of the generations, the turmoil of the crowded family, the exploitation of children, and above all, the war of the household—the misery of a lousy marriage. And there is one overriding issue that is never far from any of the others: poverty. It was also the Naturalistic drama, alongside Ibsen's, that first marked the modern theater's concern with the specific problems of women in society.

Most plays written to conform with the principles of Naturalism partook heavily of the local milieu of their settings in an effort to make the real more real. No matter where their place of origin, the plays were often buried beneath heaps of detail. The stage directions, for example, are staggeringly, almost absurdly explicit at times. Even a play as fine and as fully textured as *Vor Sonnenaufgang* makes some impossible demands on a working theater (e.g., Loth's release of a flock of pigeons from a dovectoe in Act II; there is no word about what happens during the rest of the performance in a theater filled with dozens of flying birds). All these trappings were, of course, in the interest of verisimilitude. Playwrights were convinced that the proliferation of specifics indigenous to the locale of the play and the cross section of people who lived in it were essential to putting "the truth," as opposed to nineteenth-century bombast, on the stage. Never mind that Naturalism had a romance all its own. Those of us lucky enough to have hindsight at our bidding know that most of this compulsive "realism" was probably gratuitous and, in the end, self-defeating. In their efforts to make verifiable and believable comments on the human condition as a product of heredity and environment, the Naturalists often made an inadvertently stronger case for a more provincial interpretation of their work. And the "too real" ultimately became as dated and boring as any fashionably stylized method ever had.

The essential flavor of Gerhart Hauptmann's work has always been relatively inaccessible to non-German-speaking audiences, whether in theater seats or by their reading lamps. Though a great number of his plays were widely translated, their tone and texture, even if not their denotation, remained behind an insurmountable language barrier. No dramatist knew and reproduced his historical, geographical, cultural, and linguistic milieu with greater skill than this Nobel laureate. Therein lay his greatness as well as his inaccessibility. It is hard for us today to believe how universally his genius and his influence were regarded when his plays were so quintessentially German. His unerring eye for his culture and ear for his language made his uncanny realism seem almost exotic to non-German audiences. From the beginning, the animating spirit of his words defied translation. Rendering his plays into other languages robbed them of an element crucial to their distinction. For the most part, Hauptmann remained admired and respected, but either unplayed or butchered outside the German-speaking theater. Nevertheless, despite the loss of power engendered by translation, it was always readily apparent that here was a man with much more to say than his less gifted fellow practitioners, a man with a vision penetrating far beneath surface reality, a man who did not just "take pictures" of social patterns, but who illuminated the human heart and mind.

The first edition of *Vor Sonnenaufgang*, preceding the October 1889 premiere by several months, was dedicated by Hauptmann to Bjarne P. Holmsen, "dem konsequentesten Realisten," author of the seminal Naturalistic story, *Papa Hamlet*. Holmsen was a mythical beast, the pseudonym under which *Papa Hamlet's* authors, Arno Holz and Johannes Schlaf, had published their tale. Hauptmann, in an uncharacteristic joke, apparently went along with the hoax, for he was surely one of the few who knew that Holz and Schlaf were Holmsen. Correspondence dated earlier than the dedication reveals that he was aware of the prank, and the reference to realism that was "konsequent" ("thoroughgoing") tips his hand. The phrase was central to the manifestos of Holz, Naturalism's chief German theoretician. Furthermore, "Holmsen" wasn't the "decisive" influence that the dedication would have us believe. Hauptmann was reproducing everyday speech before Holz and Schlaf. *Vor Sonnenaufgang* was probably writ-

Introduction   xv

ten, or at least underway, before *Papa Hamlet*, and Hauptmann's story *Bahnwärter Thiel* certainly predates it. The second edition of *Vor Sonnenaufgang*, issued after the explosive first performance, has a superseding dedication to the Freie Bühne in general and to its leaders, Otto Brahm and Paul Schlenther, in particular. *Vor Sonnenaufgang* was first given by the Freie Bühne one month after its highly praised performance of Ibsen's *Ghosts* and three months before its starkly Naturalistic production of Tolstoi's *Power of Darkness*. Brahm placed Hauptmann's first play in a repertoire of very select company. Twenty years later, in a gesture of honor probably coupled with nostaligia, the Freie Bühne closed its doors on 30 November 1909 with a last performance of *Vor Sonnenaufgang*.

Hauptmann's play contains all the patented thematic ingredients of German Naturalism: the struggle of people in the grip of forces beyond their control, the dramatic delineation of interacting social classes, the hard bite of economics, the concentration on workers and farmers as well as the gentry with whom they come into contact (there's a marked resemblance to *Power of Darkness*), the overweaned emphasis on heredity and environment, the frequent paralleling of the behavior of people and the beasts of the field, the deromanticized awareness of the power of sexuality, the juxtaposition of squalor and wealth living side-by-side and springing from the same conditions, the graphic depiction of the sordid and the degrading. Hauptmann had both compassion for and understanding of ordinary people, and he pioneered the dramatic presentation of their lives in modern drama. He made their destinies seem important, if for no other reason than that they are human beings entitled to some dignity; for as Chekhov was to say a bit later, "Each man is the hero of his own life." *Vor Sonnenaufgang* was not the first play of its kind, but it was the first significant one—a landmark of a dramatic form developed in the late nineteenth century that has left its imprint on the stage. Much of what we see to this day started with Hauptmann, and Hauptmann started with *Vor Sonnenaufgang*.

Among the devices Hauptmann sired was the play with a collective protagonist, the hero-less play in which the community of people whose story is being told serves as the main "character." *Die Weber* is surely his best known achievement in this vein, but *Vor Sonnenaufgang* already presents a dramatic situation in which the audience does not really identify with any single main character. The one who is most often "right," if we do not look beyond his pious pronouncements, the one whose broad social ideas might even be equated with Hauptmann's on occasion, is gratingly unsympathetic. Indeed, Alfred Loth bears a more than passing resemblance to Ibsen's Gregers Werle of

The Wild Duck (just as Schimmelpfennig clearly reminds us of Relling in that 1884 play). Hauptmann always demonstrated an inherent fairness in characterization, and Loth surely has his positive side. It is impossible not to be moved by his awareness and articulation of outrageous social injustices, and we can consider his long-range goals nothing short of admirable. An audience must share Hauptmann's own ambivalence toward his reformer, and it cannot discount what Loth says just because it may not like him personally. At the same time that we agree with and approve of Loth, we find it hard to forget that he is a narcissistic, pompous, self-righteous, humorless ass who is insensitive to the needs of others and incapable of listening to them. Ever intent on the welfare of "the people," he does not even realize when he is trampling on the feelings of the individual persons in his life. Loth is so devoted to his principles that he fails to notice that his devotion is destroying the woman he professes to love. Because he tends to exaggerate the significance of the trivial, it is hard to ascertain what is truly important to Loth. He takes all things equally seriously. Responding with a touch of paranoia most of the time, he has a talent for chronically misconstruing even the most innocent words and motives. Loth's dogged adherence to abstract values denies him any real compassion for suffering humanity; he is incapable of dealing with issues or with people as they are. Even when his thoughts and feelings are sound, he is an infuriatingly rigid fanatic. It never occurs to Alfred Loth that anything he says, does, or believes might not be correct or righteous. A salient part of his personality is Hauptmann's portrait of that peculiarly German mentality that so often has perpetrated incalculable horrors in the name of lofty (and sometimes not so lofty) principles.

Though the miseries of the poor are ever in the background of *Vor Sonnenaufgang*, they are seldom developed or made specific, as they are in *Die Weber*. Hauptmann's earlier play concentrates more on the nature of the alleged reformer than on that which, admittedly, needs to be reformed. Loth, simultaneously altruistic and egoistic, is unaware of any contradiction in his nature. He espouses and proclaims a substantial chunk of the Naturalists' philosophy of social reform, which allows Hauptmann to dramatize a far more balanced view of the points at issue than can be found in the more doctrinaire plays of his confreres and to give the play an objective texture not universally found in sociopolitical Naturalism. Hauptmann's dramatic strength was always that he concentrated on the delineation of characters rather than causes, and this strength is apparent in *Vor Sonnenaufgang* even if Loth, in his total predictability, is not as psychologically complicated as he should be. He faces no real conflict of interest at the end of the play. His choice is simple, for in leaving Helen, he remains true to himself as well as faithful to his cause. Human feeling never really enters into it. Even by his own admission, Loth is an automaton, and we never actually believe his declaration that Helen has redeemed him. That he will keep on fighting, as he says he will at the end of the play, may just be his last impotent slogan. We continue to applaud his desire to help the wretched to whom he claims to have devoted his life, but we fear that we find him wanting in his ability to do anything to right the wrongs he has properly identified and passionately described from his safe distance. Loth compels us to question the validity of a revolution that does not improve the lot of those in whose name it is generated. Most German Naturalists tended to heap uncritical praise upon such monomaniacally serious would-be redeemers and saved their scorn for bohemian rebels. Hauptmann, through his multifaceted characterization of Alfred Loth, whose principles we praise and whose behavior we deplore, gave an extra dimension of analytical honesty to his Naturalism.

Loth, the intruding socialist activist and gratuitous rocker of boats, is the catalyst of the play's dramatic action, but he is no more central to Hauptmann's overview than are the other main characters, the members of the Krause-Hoffmann household and their neighbors. The social pronouncements of many Naturalistic plays rang hollow because there was no dramatic basis in developed characters, their personal conflicts, and their relationships. Hauptmann, because he made an audience care what happened to the people in his plays, never fell into the trap.

One of the favorite subjects of late nineteenth-century German dramatists was the dissection of the ways of the nouveau riche, for a staggering number of their vulgar countrymen had fallen upon wealth in those days. The Krauses, who are country folk, and Hoffmann, the entrepreneur from the city, both illustrate the greed of those who exploited their own people as well as strangers and the faceless multitudes. Hungry for status, the trappings of culture, and the material pleasures only money could buy, they are a devastating portrait of several sorts of parvenus.

It is also interesting to compare how the play's three old comrades, fellow students in their days of rebellion of varying intensities, now view the ideals of their youth. Loth, blindly optimistic in his cause, tends to value his early activities out of all reasonable proportion to their significance. Hoffmann, always the hypocritical and cowardly self-server, denies ever having been of a persuasion other than his current stance in favor of pragmatic expediency. To him, all youthful idealism was nonsense to be outgrown; he now puts his faith in laissez faire economics and an authoritarianism he believes is benign. Dr. Schimmelpfennig, a sardonic and crafty customer, is convinced that society is irredeemably corrupt and that no real reform is possible. At best, one can help suffering individuals to endure their burdens, to make their lives, and their deaths, a bit more bearable. To this end, he works indefatigably, but never with any romantic need to martyr himself. Schimmelpfennig is convinced that not helping yourself does not necessarily help others. Yet, for all his seeming sanity and stability, Schimmelpfennig's cynicism is neither better nor worse than Loth's idealism, even if the doctor does manage to do some palpable good in contrast to Loth's windy impotence. Still, one wonders even at the end if Schimmelpfennig is to be trusted. There is no reason to believe what he tells Loth about Hoffmann and Helen, and his motives for telling it are quite suspect.

Actually, there is only one character in *Vor Sonnenaufgang* who changes in the course of the play, whose moral decisions are affected by the action of the drama. It is unfortunate that she is the least believable and most sentimentalized person in *Vor Sonnenaufgang*. Helen's power to choose is severely limited by the world in which she lives. Her only available avenues of escape from Witzdorf (is there any significance to the town's name, a *Witz* being a joke?) are marriage or death; and Loth, tantalizing her with the one, forces her to opt for the other. Nevertheless, it is only Helen who, during the play, makes a new commitment to a code of belief or conduct. Manipulated from all sides by people and circumstance, she too is ultimately impotent, but she shows herself to be the play's only true idealist, even if her idealism is totally futile and leaves us, at the final curtain, with a feeling of utter helplessness in the face of heredity and environment. Hauptmann takes great pains to demonstrate that Helen kills herself not only because of Loth's rejection but also in response to the impossibility of her whole world. Hauptmann was known to say on several occasions that he was not responsible for what his characters thought or said, that he merely let them reveal themselves truthfully. Surely, he took no sides in *Vor Sonnenaufgang*, and sometimes he seems to disapprove of all the characters almost equally; but never does he give the impression that his vision is tainted by the slightest touch of misanthropy. We get to know and understand the characters of this play. We are not asked to like them or to identify with any of them, but we are compelled to grieve for their condition.

Vor Sonnenaufgang is not an unflawed play. Though Hauptmann often expressed his desire to write plays without tidy conclusions because they were about problems that had no clear solutions, the tradition of the well-made play is still pronounced in this first work. *Vor Sonnenaufgang* has too many crude and overwrought scenes with dialogue that today sounds almost like parody. Its denouement is airtight, mechanical, and melodramatic, even if plausible. The play also abounds in retroactive exposition coming at just the opportune moment, and too often Hauptmann explains where he should reveal. The suspense of the last two acts seems somewhat contrived and does not hold, chiefly because Loth is far too intelligent to be so slow on the uptake, no matter how self-centered he may be. And too much hinges, as in Hardy's *Tess of the D'Urbervilles*, on where a letter happens to be placed. Logic would demand that Loth leave it with Schimmelpfennig, who has promised to explain to Helen. Instead, he leaves it on the table, seemingly only to facilitate the concluding action.

A more serious dramatic problem results from the functions of the two levels of plot in *Vor Sonnenaufgang*: (1) the background social conflicts at issue; (2) the central situational instability to be resolved—will Loth find out about the alcoholism in the Krause family? The latter yields the melodrama and the action of the play; the former, which is the real substance of the drama, yields the disputation within the play, its discussion and its rhetoric. *Vor Sonnenaufgang* would be a stronger drama were its main theme developed in its main action, or had Hauptmann raised fewer issues in the play and treated those in greater depth. It is easy enough to quibble with any dramatic work. Hauptmann's merits far outweigh his inadequacies in this seminal play of the modern theater, whose viability was attested to by its recent successful revival in Germany on network television, that stage that throughout the world is least hospitable to museum pieces.

No audience today would be shocked by this play, and one marvels at the vituperation it elicited in 1889. Only one year later, Wedekind's *Frühlings Erwachen* must have made *Vor Sonnenaufgang* seem both mild and conventional by comparison. But after its premiere in Berlin, antagonistic reviewers accused Hauptmann of plotlessness, coarseness, brutality, vulgarity, and downright dirtiness. So strong were some objections raised even during rehearsals that several things were deleted from the performance, such as the audibility of Martha's offstage cries in the pain of labor. Conrad Alberti, a leading critic and himself a minor playwright (who also wrote a parody of Freie Bühne fare called *Im Suff*—"Besotted"), wrote, "*Der Kot wurde in Kübeln auf die Bühne getragen, das Theater zur Mistgrube gemacht*"[1] ("It hauls filth

---

1. Conrad Alberti, "Die Freie Bühne," *Die Gesellschaft* 6 (August 1890): 1111.

onto the stage by the bucketful and turns the theater into a cesspool"). It took courage to write and to produce *Vor Sonnenaufgang* in 1889.

This play also presents an interesting sidelight for our times. After Zola, many of the more solid discoveries of nineteenth-century science found their way into literature, but they did so alongside quite a bit of hokum, particularly in the realm of heredity theory. The observers are legion who have pointed out that congenital syphilis is transmitted by the female, not the male. So much for Ibsen's *Ghosts*! (As if that changed the meaning of the play that only a fool would say is about venereal disease.) The charge most commonly leveled at *Vor Sonnenaufgang* over the years has been that too much of the play is based on the spurious premise that alcoholism runs in families not only for environmental reasons but indeed because the susceptibility to it is genetically transmitted. "Nonsense," said the psychologists. Within the past few years, geneticists have published a substantial body of evidence verifying Hauptmann's outrageous mistake, albeit three-year-old alcoholics are admittedly rare. There is apparently a genetic basis for vulnerability to alcoholism, even if environment may finish off the job. Furthermore, recent medical research reveals that there is a condition known as "alcoholic mother syndrome." Children born of alcoholic mothers who drink heavily during pregnancy have an unusually high incidence of arrested physical growth, large and small motor impairment, renal disease, and serious learning difficulties, particularly in reading. Once again, life—and even science—seem to have imitated art.

On Translating
Vor Sonnenaufgang

Hauptmann had the kind of ear for the argots of Berlin and Silesia that O'Casey and Odets had for those of Dublin and New York. And he wrote them as they sounded. Even several German editions of Hauptmann's plays are "bilingual": Silesian on the left-hand page and a "translation" into standard German on the right—hardly a good prognosis for a version that is not even in any sort of German at all.

There are already three published English translations of *Vor Sonnenaufgang*, two American and one British. Leonard Bloomfield's appeared in the magazine *Poet Lore* in 1909 and is therefore not readily available, nor need it be. It is far too frilly, genteel, bowdlerized, and uncolloquial; it reads like an interlinear "pony." The second is Ludwig Lewisohn's 1912 text from his collected edition, *The Dramatic Works of Gerhart Hauptmann*, long out of print. Lewisohn's translation, though substantially accurate, guts the play. Its entire texture is gone: the flow of the colloquial becomes stuffy and schoolbookish; the attempts at parallel English dialects call attention to themselves in their incongruity; and the purposeful vulgarities of the original text metamorphose into acceptable parlor speech. Lewisohn was a great admirer of Hauptmann, but he could not bring himself to accept, for example, that *Vor Sonnenaufgang's* most foulmouthed character is a woman. Many Germans were upset by that too, but it is the upsetting elements of this play that make it historically important. Richard Newnham's 1963 English translation for the Penguin Plays series, though smoothly natural, is too conspicuously British in diction and tone. Never distributed in the United States by its publisher, it is now also out of print in England.

For reasons extrinsic to the text, the most interesting attempt at an English translation of *Vor Sonnenaufgang* was the first one, made in the summer of 1901 by a precocious nineteen-year-old Irishman named James Joyce who was eager to improve his German at the time.[1] A

---

1. Richard Ellmann, *James Joyce* (New York: Oxford University Press, 1959), pp. 91–92.

great admirer of Ibsen and Hauptmann, Joyce hoped to persuade the Abbey Theatre to perform his *Before Sunrise*, but William Butler Yeats rejected the script in a letter that pointed out to Joyce in the kindest and most gentle phrases that his German was inadequate (and besides, Yeats could not afford to mount the play).[2] That Joyce knew the imperfections of his work all to well is clearly demonstrated by the many places in his manuscript where asterisks indicate the omission of passages he found too difficult to handle. The Silesian was more than he could manage except in its simplest manifestations, which he tried to translate into an Irish country dialect. Joyce's unpublished holograph manuscript was privately owned until the Huntington Library in California bought it at auction in 1974. His incomplete text appears in a 1975 dissertation from the University of Southern California by Jill Thompson Perkins, whose close study makes a significant contribution to Joyce scholarship and to an understanding of the impact of Naturalist drama.[3]

Hauptmann wrote dialogue appropriate to the characters in his play—high German for the educated, Berliner patois for the common folk from the city, rural Silesian for the miners and farmers. Even the peasants have subtly differentiated levels of diction depending on whether they are landed farmers or hired hands, young or old, field laborers or village tradesmen. German usage in *Vor Sonnenaufgang* ranges from Loth and Schimmelpfennig's intellectually articulate level of banter and disputation down to the groping pauses, fragments, unfinished phrases, faulty references of pronouns, and grammatical mayhem of the maids and hands. Hauptmann never writes dialogue that asks a speaker to demonstrate language skill beyond his station. In translating Hauptmann, one dare not clean up the syntax or put phrases into mouths accustomed to grunting monosyllables, and this creates a problem if the translator decides not to lean on any identifiable dialects at all. There is no English or American equivalent to Silesian or any other local dialect, German or otherwise. "Early Teutonic Tobacco Road" will not do; it invariably sounds silly and jarringly out of place. The only way to let the play remain German yet capture the importance of the characters' clearly different ways of speaking (and all that these differences imply in terms of social comment) is to do with levels of diction in English what Hauptmann does with dialects in German, and to make the dialogue convincingly

---

2. Ibid., pp. 183–84, quoting Yeats's letter to Joyce, which is in the Slocum Collection at Yale University.

3. Jill Thompson Perkins, *Joyce and Hauptmann: "Before Sunrise"* (San Marino, Calif.: Huntington Library Publications, 1978).

colloquial while avoiding English phrases peculiar to a particular place or time. That no one, not even the theatrically experienced and colloquially bilingual like myself, has translated this important play successfully in its almost ninety years should have served as a warning. Instead, it became a challenge.

There remains only the need to explain why I decided on the title *Before Daybreak* rather than on more obvious alternatives. *Before Dawn* is too soft and smacks of something that should grace your favorite network between 3:30 and 4:00 P.M. each Monday through Friday. *Before Sunrise* calls up images of an obsequious chaplain, a last cigarette, and a declined blindfold. And *Before Sun-Up* evokes a vision of the gathering of the hands in preparation for the great dogie drive to Laramie. *Before Daybreak* sounds right to me, and in translating Hauptmann, the rightness of the sound is everything.

A Note On The Text

Vor Sonnenaufgang was written in 1889 and was first published in that same year by C. F. Conrads Buchhandlung in Berlin. In contrast to British and American custom, it is not unusual for a play to be published in Germany before it is performed.

The first edition bore the following dedication:

Dedicated to that most painstaking of realists, Bjarne P. Holmsen, author of *Papa Hamlet*, in joyful recognition of the decisively stimulating influence of his book.

Erkner   Gerhart Hauptmann
8 July 1889

The second edition, prepared shortly after the play's premiere, contained the following additional prefatory remark:

This drama was first performed on 20 October at the Lessing Theater under the auspices of the Free Stage Society [Verein Freie Bühne]. I take the opportunity afforded by this new edition to give my most heartfelt thanks to all the leaders of that society, but most especially to Messrs. Otto Brahm and Paul Schlenther. May the future prove that by defying petty considerations and by helping to give life to a work that had its origin in pure motives, they have brought honor to German art and to themselves.

Charlottenburg   Gerhart Hauptmann
26 October 1889

The text for this translation is that of the *Centenar-Ausgabe*, Hauptmann's collected works, published in honor of the hundredth anniversary of his birth (15 November 1962) by the Propyläen Verlag and edited by Hans-Egon Hass. However, since the convention of indicating stage directions in English is to let L. and R. mean stage left and stage right, L. and R. have been reversed from the original to conform with the customary English style. A very few minor interpolations in the stage directions are in the interest of clarity in translation and have been enclosed in brackets.

Before Daybreak

A Social Drama

by

Gerhart Hauptmann

Translated by Peter Bauland

Acts I, III, V

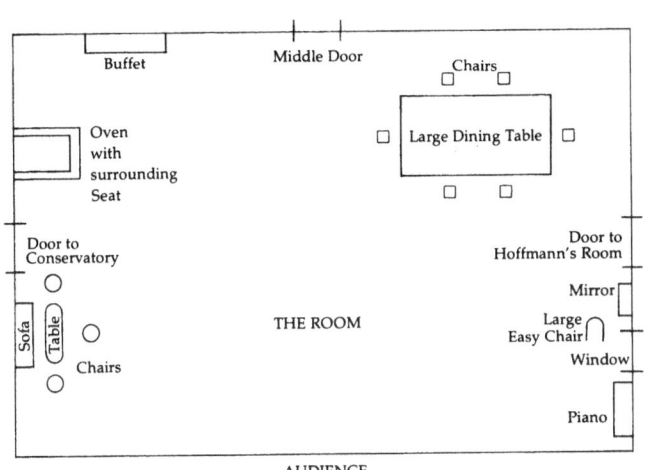

Acts II, IV

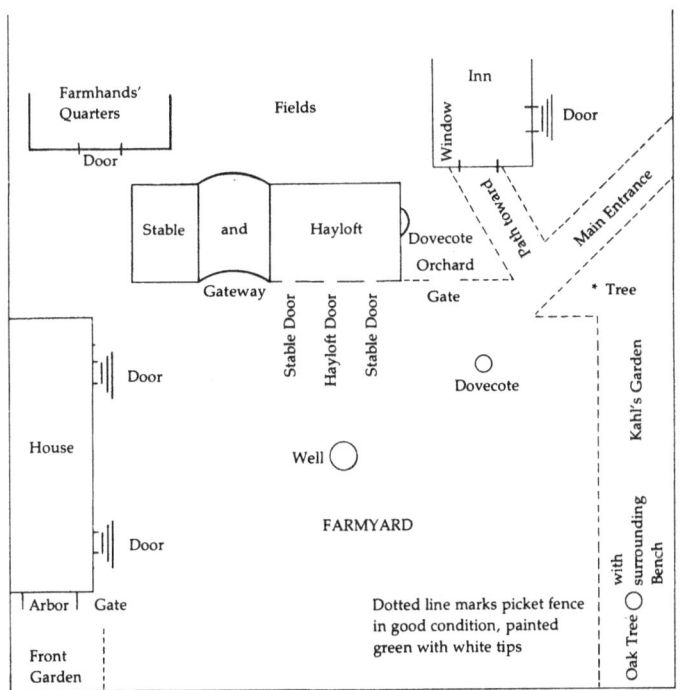

Dramatis Personae

KRAUSE, farmlandowner

MRS. KRAUSE, his second wife

HELEN \
 } Krause's daughters by his first marriage
MARTHA /

HOFFMANN, engineer, married to Martha

WILLIAM KAHL, Mrs. Krause's nephew

MRS. SPILLER, companion to Mrs. Krause

ALFRED LOTH

DR. SCHIMMELPFENNIG

BEIBST, hired hand on Krause's farm

GUSTE \
LIESE } maidservants on Krause's farm
MARIE /

BAER, known as "Hoppy Baer"

EDWARD, Hoffmann's servant

MIELE, Mrs. Krause's housemaid

THE COACHMAN'S WIFE

GOLISCH, cowherd

A PARCEL DELIVERY MAN

Act I

The room has a low ceiling; its floors are covered with rugs of quality. Modern extravagance seems to be crammed into a place suited to peasant sparseness. On the wall behind the dining table, there is a picture of a wagon pulled by four horses being driven by a carter in a blue tunic.

MIELE, a robust peasant girl with a red and rather stupid looking face, opens the middle door upstage, allowing ALFRED LOTH to enter. Loth is of medium height, broad-shouldered, stocky, decisive but a bit clumsy in his movements. He has blond hair, blue eyes, and a thin, light little moustache. His bony face bears a constantly serious expression. He is conservatively but nevertheless fashionably dressed: topcoat, shoulder-strap bag, walking stick.

MIELE. Please, come in. I'll call Mr. Hoffmann right away. Have a seat, won't you?

The glass door leading to the conservatory is thrown open with a vengeance; a peasant woman, her face bluish red with rage, hurls herself inside. She is dressed not much better than a washerwoman: bare, red arms; blue cotton skirt and bodice; red polka-dotted neckerchief. She is in her early forties; her face is hard, sensual, malevolent. Otherwise, her figure is well preserved.

MRS. KRAUSE. *(Screams.)* You sluts!! . . . Honest to God, I never seen scum the like o' you girls! . . . *(To Loth.)* Shove off! You don't get nothin' here! . . . *(Half to Miele, half to Loth.)* He got arms, he can work. Get out! Nobody gets no handouts!
LOTH. But, Madame, you can't possibly think that . . . look, my name is Loth . . . I'm . . . I want to . . . I haven't the slightest inten—. . .
MIELE. He only wants to talk to Mr. Hoffmann.
MRS. KRAUSE. Oh, he wants to put the touch on my son-in-law, does he? We know all about that sort o' thing! He ain't got nothin' that's his neither. Anythin' he's got, he's got from us.

The door to HOFFMANN'S room (L.) is opened. He sticks his head in.

HOFFMAN. Mother! I must really ask you . . . *(He enters, turns to Loth.)* What can I do for . . . Alfred! My old friend! Well, I'll be damned. It's really you. What a pleasant surprise.

Hoffmann is about thirty-three, slim, tall, haggard. He is dressed in the latest fad of fashion, is elegantly barbered, wears expensive rings, has diamond studs in his shirt and gaudy pendants on his watch chain. His hair is black, as is his moustache which is luxurious and most carefully pampered. His features are sharp and birdlike, but his expression is vague. At times, his dark bright eyes are restless.

LOTH. Actually, it's quite by accident that . . .
HOFFMANN. *(Excited.)* Nothing nicer could . . . But, first things first. Take your things off! *(He tries to help him off with his shoulder bag.)* Nothing nicer . . . or so unexpected—*(He has taken Loth's hat and cane and places them on a chair by the door.)*—could in any way have happened to me right now . . . *(Returning.)* Nothing . . . really nothing.
LOTH. *(Removing the shoulder bag himself.)* Actually, it really *is* quite by accident that I've . . . *(He places the bag on the table downstage.)*
HOFFMANN. Sit down. You must be exhausted. Please—sit down. Do you still remember when you used to come to see me? You always flopped yourself down on the sofa so that the springs creaked . . . and occasionally busted. Hey, listen! Do it the way you used to.

Mrs. Krause's face has been registering great astonishment, and she withdraws. Loth sits down on one of the chairs surrounding the table downstage.

HOFFMANN. Have a drink. What'll you have? . . . Beer? Wine? Cognac? Coffee? Tea? We have everything.

HELEN enters from the conservatory, reading. Her tall, slightly too plump body, the style of her unusually abundant blond hair, the expression on her face, her modern clothing, her way of moving, her entire appearance cannot quite hide that she is a country girl.

HELEN. Brother, you might . . . *(She discovers Loth and pulls back quickly.)* Oh, I beg your pardon. *(Exit.)*
HOFFMANN. Stay here; please do!
LOTH. Your wife?
HOFFMANN. No; her sister. Didn't you hear what she called me?

LOTH. No.
HOFFMANN. Pretty, isn't she? . . . Well, come on, what will it be? Coffee? Tea? Grog?
LOTH. No, nothing at all. Thank you.
HOFFMANN. *(Offers cigars.)* Then here's something to entice you, no?! . . . Not even this?
LOTH. No, thank you.
HOFFMANN. Enviable lack of self-indulgence! *(He lights a cigar for himself while speaking.)* The ashes . . . rather, the . . . the tobacco . . . mnnn . . . that is to say the smoke, of course . . . doesn't bother you, does it?
LOTH. No.
HOFFMANN. Good God, if I didn't still have at least *this* little bit of pleasure! . . . But, do me a favor now, huh? Tell me something about yourself. Ten years—and, by the way, you've hardly changed—ten years—a distressing chunk of time. How's Schn . . . Schnurz? That's what we called him, wasn't it? And Fips, and the whole happy crew from way back then? Have you kept in touch with any of them?
LOTH. You mean to say you don't know?
HOFFMANN. What?
LOTH. That he shot himself.
HOFFMANN. Who? *Now* who's gone and shot himself?
LOTH. Fips! Friedrich Hildebrandt.
HOFFMANN. I don't believe it.
LOTH. Fact! He blew his brains out—in Grunewald Park,[1] in an exceedingly lovely spot on the shore of Lake Havel.[2] I've been there. Has a fine view of Spandau.[3]
HOFFMANN. Hmmnnn. Never thought he'd do such a thing. He was never the heroic sort.
LOTH. That's exactly why he shot himself.—He was conscientious, very conscientious.
HOFFMANN. Conscientious? What do you mean?
LOTH. Well, for that very reason . . . otherwise he probably wouldn't have shot himself.
HOFFMANN. I still don't follow you.
LOTH. Well, surely you know the color of the political views he held.
HOFFMANN. Certainly. Green!
LOTH. It's easy for you to say that, but you'll have to admit that he was

---

1. A large park in Berlin.
2. A lake within the city limits of Berlin.
3. A section of Berlin.

a conspicuously gifted young man. And yet, for five years he had to grind away as a stucco-worker—and for another five he was independently poor, starving along on his own hook, as it were, all the while moulding those little clay statues of his.

HOFFMANN. And was that stuff ever repulsive! I like art that cheers me up. . . . No, his kind of art wasn't at all my taste.

LOTH. Nor mine; but he had faith in it, stuck up for it obstinately. Last spring there was an open competition for a commission. I believe some petty prince or other was supposed to get a monument to assure his immortality. Fips entered—and he won. Shortly thereafter, he shot himself.

HOFFMANN. What that has to do with his alleged conscientiousness escapes me. As far as I'm concerned, it's just plain nonsense.—It's crazy—contrary—capricious.

LOTH. That's the general consensus.

HOFFMANN. I'm sorry, but I can't help subscribing to it.

LOTH. Well, what difference can it make to Fips now what people think of . . .

HOFFMANN. Oh, let's drop it anyhow. Actually, I feel just as sorry for him as you do. But now he's gone, dead; he was a fine fellow. . . . Why don't you tell me something about yourself instead? What you've been doing—how the world's been treating you.

LOTH. It's been treating me as I expected it to. . . . Haven't you heard anything about me at all? I mean, in the papers?

HOFFMANN. *(A bit embarrassed.)* Wouldn't know what.

LOTH. Nothing of the business in Leipzig?

HOFFMANN. Oh, that! Well, yes . . . I think . . . but nothing specific.

LOTH. Well, then, it went something like this—

HOFFMANN. *(Laying his hand on Loth's arm.)* Before you begin, can't I get you anything at all?

LOTH. Later, maybe.

HOFFMANN. Not even a little glass of cognac?

LOTH. No. That least of all.

HOFFMANN. Well, I'll have a small . . . nothing's better for your digestion. *(He gets a bottle and two little glasses from the buffet upstage R. and places them on the table in front of Loth.)* Grand Champagne, best brand you can get; I recommend it. Won't you . . . ?

LOTH. No, thank you.

HOFFMANN. *(Downs a glassful.)* Aaaahh—that's better! Now—I'm all ears.

LOTH. In a word, I got myself into quite a mess.

HOFFMANN. They gave you two years, didn't they?

LOTH. Precisely. Seems you know about it after all. Two years in jail, and then to top it off, they expelled me from the university. I was just twenty-one. It was during those two years that I wrote my first book on economics, but I'd be lying if I said that it was actually a pleasure to be behind bars.

HOFFMANN. My God, what a bunch of fools we were. Strange! We thought and planned all those things in dead earnest. I can't help saying it now—it was sheer childishness. We were going to go to America. We! Us! A dozen green youngsters—and *we* were going to establish a model state. What a joke!

LOTH. Childishness?! Well, in some ways it really was; we underestimated the difficulties of such an enterprise.

HOFFMANN. And to think that you really went all the way out there—to America—in all seriousness, and without a penny to your name. Think about it: what it means to believe you can acquire the land and the basic essentials for a model state when you're standing there empty-handed. That was close to insane . . . In any case, it was spectacularly naive.

LOTH. Yet, it's the result of my trip to America that I find particularly satisfying.

HOFFMANN. *(With a burst of laughter.)* What? Like a cold shower? If you mean it that way, the results were excellent.

LOTH. Could be that it cooled me down somewhat, but that doesn't make me unique. The cooling down process is something we all have to go through. Still, it's a far cry from acknowledging that fact to underestimating the value of our—let's call them our hot-blooded days. And they weren't as dreadfully naive as you make them out to be.

HOFFMANN. Well, I'm not so sure about that.

LOTH. All you need to do is consider the average brand of nonsense that was all around us back then: the fraternity drivel going on at the universities, the boozing, the duelling. Why all the noise? For Hecuba, as Fips used to say. Well, at least we didn't get all worked up for Hecuba; we aimed for the highest, the most idealistic goals of humanity. Moreover, those naive days wiped out all my prejudices. I divested myself of sham religion, sham morality, and a lot of other . . .

HOFFMANN. Granted! If, when all's said and done, I am an objective and enlightened man today, I owe it—and I'd never deny that—to the days of our boon companionship.—Naturally!—I'd be the last to deny that. I'm a reasonable man, you know. But you can't beat your head against the wall. You can't wipe out the ills and evils from which our generation unfortunately suffers by replacing them with worse ones. You have to let everything take its natural course.

Whatever will be, will be! You've got to be practical, practical! And, remember! I used to emphasize that then as now. And that principle has paid off for me. That's the way it is. The rest of you—you included—are all manifestly *im*practical.

LOTH. Would you mind explaining what you mean by that?

HOFFMANN. Easy! You don't exploit your abilities. You, for instance—a man like you—with brains, energy, and so forth. What doors wouldn't have been open to you? But, no! What do you do instead? You compromise yourself, right at the start, to such a degree that . . . Now, tell the truth, didn't you regret it every once in a while?

LOTH. I couldn't very well regret that I was condemned innocently.

HOFFMANN. I can't be the judge of that, you know.

LOTH. Yes, you can, and right now, when I've told you that the indictment declared that I created our "Vancouver Island Society" purely for purposes of political agitation. Also that I solicited funds for partisan purposes. You know very well that we were serious in our endeavor of founding a colony, and as far as the matter of soliciting money goes, you yourself said that we were collectively penniless. There wasn't a shred of truth in the entire indictment, and as a member of the group, you ought to . . .

HOFFMANN. Wait a minute. I wasn't actually a member. Furthermore, it goes without saying that I believe you. After all, judges are only human. In any case, in order to deal with the matter practically, you should have avoided even the appearance of such a thing. Altogether, I've wondered a good bit about you since then: editor of *The Worker's Tribune*, the most insignificant little radical rag . . . and then, the stinking rabble's own candidate for parliament. And what do you have to show for it? Don't get me wrong! I'd be the last man short on sympathy for the common folk, but if anything is going to be made to happen, it must be made to happen from above. From above is, in fact, the only way to get anything done. The people never know what's good for them. It's all this voice-of-the-people, will-of-the-people hogwash of yours that I call beating your head against the wall.

LOTH. I'm afraid I can't quite make out what you're driving at.

HOFFMANN. What I'm driving at is this: Look at me! My hands are neither tied nor empty. I'm in a position to do something about my ideals. It's safe to say that I've completed the practical aspect of my plans. But you and the others—always empty-handed—what can you do?

LOTH. Yes, the word is that you're well on your way to becoming a regular Rothschild.[4]

HOFFMANN. *(Flattered.)* An overstatement—at least for the time being. Who says so, anyway? A man works hard and plods onward from day to day, and that, naturally, has its rewards. . . . Now, really, who said that?

LOTH. I was over in Jauer.[5] Two men were discussing it at the next table.

HOFFMANN. Hey, listen! I *do* have enemies! What did they have to say?

LOTH. Nothing special. I just heard them say that for the present, you had retired to the estate of your in-laws.

HOFFMANN. Honestly, the way people go sniffing around! You wouldn't believe how a man in my position is spied on wherever he turns. That's another one of the drawbacks of having mon— . . . Actually, it's this way: it's quiet here and the air is clean; I thought it would be a good place for my wife to deliver the baby.

LOTH. What do you do for a doctor? A good physician is of the utmost importance in childbirth, and in a backwater town such as this . . .

HOFFMANN. That's just it! The doctor here is an unusually capable one. And, you know, this much I've learned: in a physician, conscientiousness counts for more than genius.

LOTH. Maybe it's the natural by-product of genius in a doctor.

HOFFMANN. Could be. In any case, our doctor is conscientious. He's a bit of an idealist, too—more or less our type. He's had fantastic success with the miners and peasants. They worship him. Sometimes he's hard to take; he's a curious mixture of hard-boiled and sentimental. But, as I said, I know conscientiousness when I see it . . . absolutely!—Oh, before I forget . . . this is important to me . . . a man always ought to know what he has to be on the lookout for. . . . Listen . . . tell me . . . I can see it in your face. Those men at the next table didn't have anything good to say about me, did they? What *did* they say? Please, tell me.

LOTH. I really shouldn't, because I'm just about to beg you for 200 Marks . . . literally beg, because there's hardly a chance that I'll ever be able to pay you back.

HOFFMANN. *(Pulls a checkbook from the breast pocket of his coat, makes out a*

---

4. In Hauptmann's text, Loth refers to "Bleichröder," not "Rothschild," but since the wealthy and powerful Berlin banking house of Bleichröder is virtually unknown today, particularly outside of Germany (but also within it), I have taken the liberty of substituting a name that an English-speaking audience would recognize immediately and that conveys the sense of the line.

5. A small city west of Breslau in Silesia, Jauer was in Germany at the time of the play. Like most of Silesia, it became a part of Poland after World War II. Jauer is now known as Jawor.

check and hands it to Loth.) Cash it at any branch of the Imperial Bank. . . . Let it be my pleasure . . .

LOTH. You're even quicker than I dared hope you'd be. Well, I accept gratefully, and you know—you're not exactly making a bad investment.

HOFFMANN. *(With a touch of pompousness.)* A laborer is worthy of his hire!—But now, Loth, do me a favor: what did the men at that table . . . ?

LOTH. I'm sure they were talking utter nonsense.

HOFFMANN. Tell me anyway . . . please! I'm simply interested, just interested—nothing more.

LOTH. It had to do with some contractor named Müller—. They said that you muscled him out of his position here.

HOFFMANN. Stands to reason! Same old story!

LOTH. I think they said he was supposed to have been engaged to your wife.

HOFFMANN. That he was. Anything else?

LOTH. I'm telling you everything just as I heard it. I assume it's important to you that you know exactly how you're being slandered.

HOFFMANN. Absolutely correct. So?

LOTH. As far as I could make out, this Müller contracted to build a stretch of the mountain railroad here.

HOFFMANN. Right! And with a measly ten thousand for starting capital. When he realized that the money wasn't going to stretch far enough, he tried to make a quick catch of some available daughter of any of the local landowners. The woman I later married drew the lucky number.

LOTH. They said that he courted the daughter with success, but that you had managed to woo the old man.—Then Müller shot himself, didn't he? The story is that you even took over his contract, finished the construction, and to top it off, made a tidy sum on the transaction. Right?

HOFFMANN. There's an element of truth in that, but I could give you an altogether different interpretation of the circumstances from my perspective. Did they have any other edifying things to say?

LOTH. There was one thing, I must tell, that particularly enraged them: they tallied up what tremendous business you were doing in coal right now, and they called you a . . . well, it wasn't exactly flattering. In a word, they said that over some champagne, you convinced the yokels around here to sign a contract that gave you the exclusive marketing rights to all the coal mined on their property in return for a fantastically small assured rental fee.

Act I

HOFFMANN. *(Visibly distressed and embarrassed, rises.)* Let me tell you something, Loth . . . Oh, why should we bother ourselves with this at all? Tell you what: let's think about supper instead. I've got a murderous appetite—I am monstrously hungry. *(He presses a button attached to a green cord hanging above the sofa. A buzzer sounds offstage.)*
LOTH. Well, if you'd like me to stay, I'd appreciate it if I might wash up a bit first.
HOFFMANN. You'll have everything you need in a moment.
(EDWARD, a liveried servant, enters.) Edward, show the gentleman to the guest room.
EDWARD. Very good, sir!
HOFFMANN. *(Pressing Loth's hand.)* Would you mind coming down for supper in about fifteen minutes at the latest?
LOTH. More than enough time. See you later.
HOFFMANN. Good. See you soon.

Edward opens the door and allows Loth to precede him. Both exit. Hoffmann scratches the back of his head, looks pensively at the floor, then heads toward the door to his room, L. He has just grasped the knob when Helen, who has entered quickly by the glass door R., calls to him.

HELEN. Brother! Who was that?
HOFFMANN. That was one of my friends from school—as a matter of fact, my oldest friend, Alfred Loth.
HELEN. *(Quickly.)* Has he left already?
HOFFMANN. No. He's going to have supper with us. Maybe . . . just maybe . . . he'll spend the night.
HELEN. Oh, Jesus! Then I'm not coming to supper.
HOFFMANN. Well, why not, Helen?
HELEN. What's the sense of me meeting educated people? Just let me keep on growing peacefully rustic around here.
HOFFMANN. Oh, please, not that old song and dance again! In fact, you'll do me the great favor of ordering the supper arrangements, won't you? Let's make it a bit festive. I suspect he has something up his sleeve.
HELEN. What do you mean "up his sleeve"?
HOFFMANN. Sniffing. Probing. Rooting around like a mole. He's trying to dig something up. Nothing you'd know about. Of course, I might be wrong, because so far I've been able to avoid raising the subject. In any event, make everything as cozy and enticing as possible; that's that easiest way to get people to . . . well, anyway—. Champagne, of course. Have the lobsters come from Hamburg?

HELEN. This morning, I think.
HOFFMANN. Fine! Then—lobsters! *(A loud knocking at the door.)* Come in.
PARCEL DELIVERY MAN. *(Enters with fairly large package under his arm. Speaks in sing-song voice.)* Paaack-age.
HELEN. Where from?
MAN. Ber-li-in.
HOFFMANN. Right! Must be the baby outfit from Hertzog's *(He looks at the package and takes the bill.)* Yes, it is the stuff from Hertzog's.
HELEN. This whole crateful? You're overdoing things.

Hoffmann pays the delivery man.

MAN. *(Still half-singing.)* Have yourselves a good eeeve-ning. *(Exit.)*
HOFFMANN. Why is that overdoing things?
HELEN. Why? Because there must be enough here to outfit at least three babies.
HOFFMANN. Did you take a walk with my wife?
HELEN. What can I do? She always gets tired right away!
HOFFMANN. Oh, good grief!—Tired right away! She's really starting to get me down. An hour-and-a-half . . . why, for Chris'sake, won't she do what the doctor tells her to? What do we have a doctor for anyway, if . . .
HELEN. Then put your foot down and get that Spiller woman out of here! What can I do against an old hag like that who keeps encouraging every silly idea Martha gets?
HOFFMANN. What about me—a man? What can I do? Besides that, you know my mother-in-law, don't you?
HELEN. *(Bitterly.)* I certainly do.
HOFFMANN. Where is she now?
HELEN. Old lady Spiller's been getting her all decked out in her finery ever since Mr. Loth's been here. Come suppertime, she'll probably treat us to one of her spectacular performances.
HOFFMANN. *(Wrapped up in his own thoughts again. Paces about the room; furious.)* So help me, this is the last time I put up with this sort of thing—the last time in this house, I promise you.
HELEN. You're lucky. You can go anywhere you please.
HOFFMANN. In my own home, this unfortunate relapse into that horrible vice would certainly not have happened.
HELEN. Don't blame me! I didn't give her the brandy! Just get rid of that Spiller woman. If only I were a man!
HOFFMANN. *(Sighing.)* Oh, if only it were all over and done with! *(From the door, L.)* Anyway, Helen, do me the favor, will you: a really

appetizing supper. There's just a little something I must attend to in the meantime. [*Exit.*]

HELEN. *(Pushes the buzzer. Miele enters.)* Miele, set the table, and tell Edward to put champagne on ice and open four dozen oysters.

MIELE. *(Put-upon, sassy.)* Ya c'n tell 'im y'rself. He don't take no orders from me. Sez 'e was hired by Mr. Hoffmann.

HELEN. Then, at least, send him in. *(Miele goes. Helen steps in front of the mirror, straightens several trifling details of her appearance. Edward enters. Helen, still before the mirror.)* Edward, put champagne on ice and open some oysters. Mr. Hoffmann's orders.

EDWARD. Very good, Miss. *(Exit Edward. Immediately thereafter, a knock at the middle door, upstage.)*

HELEN. *(Startled.)* Oh, my God! *(Timidly.)* Come in! *(Louder and more resolutely.)* Come in!

LOTH. *(Enters without bowing.)* Oh! Sorry! I didn't mean to disturb you. My name is Loth.

Helen curtseys—dancing school style.

HOFFMANN. *(His voice heard through the closed door to his room.)* Hey, children! No formalities! I'll be right out. Loth, my sister-in-law, Helen Krause! Helen, my friend, Alfred Loth. Consider yourselves properly introduced.

HELEN. Oh, really, what kind of . . .

LOTH. That doesn't bother me. Everyone keeps telling me that as far as etiquette is concerned, I'm a semibarbarian myself.—But, if I disturbed you, I . . .

HELEN. Please—you didn't at all—I assure you. *(Embarrassed pause. Then.)* It's . . . it's . . . nice of you to have looked up my brother-in-law. He often complains that . . . that is, he's so sad that his old friends seem to have forgotten him completely.

LOTH. Yes, this has all been a happy accident. I've always been in and around Berlin—had no idea where Hoffmann had been keeping himself. I haven't been back in Silesia since I was a student at Breslau.[6]

HELEN. So, you stumbled upon him by sheer coincidence?

LOTH. Only that—and what's more, in the very place where I have to pursue my research.

HELEN. Here in Witzdorf? That's impossible; you can't be serious. Research in this godforsaken hole?

---

6. A major city just above the fifty-first parallel in the eastern reaches of Germany at the time of the play and until 1945, Breslau now falls within the Polish border and is known as Wroclaw.

LOTH. "Godforsaken," you call it? Yet there is an extraordinary degree of wealth to be found here.

HELEN. Oh, *that*, of course, but . . .

LOTH. I find it constantly amazing. I can assure you that such farms cannot be found anywhere else; affluence seems to spill out of every door and window.

HELEN. You're right about that. There's more than one stable around here in which cows and horses feed from marble troughs and nickel hayracks. We can thank all the coal found under our fields for that. It made some poor peasants monumentally rich overnight. *(She points to the picture on the rear wall.)* Look at that. My grandfather drove a cart. This little plot of land here was his, but he couldn't eke a living out of such a patch of dirt, so he had to haul freight on the side. That's him in his blue tunic—they still wore such things in those days. When my father was young, he wore one too. No, I didn't mean it that way when I said "godforsaken." It's just that it's so dreary around here. There's absolutely nothing to nourish mind or spirit. It's enough to bore you to death.

Miele and Edward bustle back and forth in the background as they set the table, upstage L.

LOTH. Aren't there dances or parties now and then?

HELEN. Not even that. The farmers are busy gambling, hunting, drinking. . . . What is there to look at the livelong day? *(She has gone to the window and points out.)* Creatures like that, mainly.

LOTH. Hmmmn. Miners.

HELEN. Some are going to the pits; some are coming from the pits. It never ends.—At least I always get to see miners. Do you think I even want to walk out in the streets alone? With a little luck, I get to slip out the back gate and into the fields once in a while. They're such a crude pack—and the way they keep staring at you—so ominously and half-threatening—as if you were guilty of something. Sometimes, in the winter, when we go in the sleigh, we can see huge gangs of them coming over the hills through the darkness, with the wind swirling the snow around them. Instead of getting out of the way, they keep trudging onward right in front of the horses. Then, sometimes, the farmers reach for their whips; it's the only way they can get through. Then the miners curse us from behind. Sometimes I've been so dreadfully frightened.

LOTH. What would you think if I told you that it is for the sake of these very people who terrify you that I have come here?

HELEN. You can't mean . . .

LOTH. I'm dead serious. They interest me more than anyone else around here.
HELEN. With no exceptions?
LOTH. None.
HELEN. Not even my brother-in-law?
LOTH. No! My interest in these people is of an entirely different . . . of a higher significance. . . . You must excuse me, Miss Krause, but I can't expect you to grasp what I'm driving at.
HELEN. Why not? I understand very well. You . . . *(She allows a letter to slip from her pocket. Loth bends down to retrieve it.)* Oh, don't bother. It's unimportant. Just a note from a boarding school girlfriend.
LOTH. You went to boarding school?
HELEN. Yes. In Herrnhut.[7] You needn't think that I'm completely . . . No, I think I do understand what you mean.
LOTH. What I mean is that these workers interest me for their own sake.
HELEN. Yes, of course. A miner can be very interesting, if you look at it that way. I mean, after all, there are parts of the country where you never get to see one, but when you have them all around you, day in, day out . . .
LOTH. Even if you do have them all around you, Miss Krause. In fact, it is imperative that we see them daily in order to discover that which is truly interesting about them.
HELEN. Well, if it's all that hard to discover . . . I mean, what is it, anyway, that's so interesting?
LOTH. It is, for example, interesting that these people, as you say, always look so menacing or ominous.
HELEN. Why do you think that's especially interesting?
LOTH. Because it's out of the ordinary. The rest of us may have that look once in a while, but by no means always.
HELEN. Then, why *do* they always look so . . . so surly, so full of hatred? There has to be a reason for it.
LOTH. Precisely! And that reason is exactly what I want to find out.
HELEN. Oh, really now. You're making all this up. What good would it do you even if you knew?
LOTH. It might make it possible to find a way to get rid of whatever it is that makes these people so joyless and so full of hatred. It might even be possible to make them happier.
HELEN. *(A bit confused.)* I must tell you, quite honestly, that . . . and yet, just now, maybe I do begin to understand you a very little. Only, it's all so new to me—so very new.

---

7. A Saxonian town near Dresden, Herrnhut is now in the German Democratic Republic (East Germany).

HOFFMANN. *(Entering through his door, L. He has several letters in his hand.)* Well, here I am again.—Edward! These letters have to be at the post office before eight. *(He hands the letters to the servant, who exits.)* So, folks, now we can eat!—Unbearably hot here! September, and this kind of heat! *(He lifts a bottle of champagne from the ice bucket.)* Veuve Cliquot; Edward knows my secret passions. *(Turns to Loth.)* Had yourselves a lively little argument, didn't you? *(Goes over to the table, now fully set and ostentatiously laden with delicacies. Rubs his hands.)* Well, that looks pretty good. *(With a sly look toward Loth.)* Don't you think so, too?—Oh, by the way, Helen—we're going to have company: William Kahl. I just saw him out in the yard.

HELEN. *(Makes an unmannerly gesture of revulsion.)*

HOFFMANN. Oh, please, dear. You're acting almost as if I . . . How can I help it? You don't think he's here at *my* invitation? *(Heavy footsteps can be heard in the hall.)* Fee-Fi-Fo-Fum! Disaster comes on plodding feet!

KAHL enters without having bothered to knock. He is twenty-four, a clumsy clodhopper of a peasant obviously doing his meager best to give the illusion of being not only refined, but also rich. His features are coarse; his dominant expression is one of stupid cunning. He wears a green jacket, a multicolored velvet vest, dark trousers, and patent leather knee boots. His hat is of the green Tyrolean hunter's variety with appropriate plumage. His jacket has buttons of stag's horn, his watch chain is adorned with stag's teeth, and so forth. He stutters.

KAHL. G-g-good evenin', folks. *(He sees Loth, becomes quite embarrassed, stands still, and is a rather sorry sight.)*

HOFFMANN. *(Walks over to him and shakes his hand cheerfully.)* Good evening, Mr. Kahl.

HELEN. *(Ungraciously.)* Evening.

KAHL. *(Lumbers right across the entire room to Helen and shakes her hand.)* Evenin' t'you too, Nellie.

HOFFMANN. *(To Loth.)* May I introduce our neighbor's son, Mr. Kahl.

KAHL. *(Grins; tugs at and turns the hat in his hand. Awkward silence.)*

HOFFMANN. All right, then children—let's sit down! Anyone still missing? Ah, yes—our beloved mother-in-law. Miele! Please ask Mrs. Krause to come to the table.

Miele exits through the middle door.

MIELE. *(Out in the hall. Yelling.)* Missus!!—Hey, Missus!! Time to come down!—So, come on down!!

Helen and Hoffmann exchange glances; they understand, and they laugh. Then both look at Loth.

HOFFMANN. *(To Loth.)* "Other countries; other customs."

MRS. KRAUSE appears, dreadfully overdressed. Lots of shiny silk and expensive jewelry. Both bearing and garb betray callous arrogance, absurd vanity, and the pride born of stupidity.

HOFFMANN. Ah, there you are, Mother! Permit me to introduce my friend, Dr. Loth.
MRS. KRAUSE. *(Improvises a grotesque curtsey.)* Pleased-t'meetcha. *(After a short pause.)* Now first, Doctor, I gotta ask ya not to have no hard feelin's toward me, 'n I'm properly sorry, so 'scuse me, will ya?—'Scuse me on account o' the way I acted afore. *(The longer she speaks, the faster she speaks.)* Y'know, y'unnerstan', we got a whoppin' big bunch o' bums comes bummin' their way in 'n outa these parts. . . . Ya wouldn' believe the kind o' trouble we got with them moochers. Bunch o' magpies'll swipe anythin' ain't nailed down. An' it ain't 'zackly 's if we was tight, ya know. A penny one way or t'other don't mean nothin' to us . . . or a Mark neither. Not on yer life! Now, you take Ludwig Krause's ol' lady, she's 's cheap 's they come; wouldn' give ya th' time o' day. Her ol' man dropped dead in a fit o' rage 'cause he lost a lousy two thousan' playin' cards. Well, we ain't that sort, ya know. See that buffet over there? Set me back two hunnert—'n that don't even include the shippin' costs. Baron Klinkow himself ain't got nothin' better.

MRS. SPILLER has also entered, shortly after Mrs. Krause. She is small, somewhat deformed, and decked out in Mrs. Krause's hand-me-downs. While Mrs. Krause speaks, she looks up at her with a kind of admiration. She is about fifty-five. Her breath is accompanied by a quiet little moan when she exhales; it is regularly audible, even when she speaks, as a soft "nnngg."

MRS. SPILLER. *(In an obsequious, affectedly melancholic, minor-key tone. Very softly.)* His Lordship the Baron has the exact same buffet—nnngg—.
HELEN. *(To Mrs. Krause.)* Mother, don't you think we should sit down before we . . .

MRS. KRAUSE. *(With a lightning fast turn to Helen, and a scathing look; brusquely and imperiously.)* Izzat fittin' 'n proper? *(She is just about to sit down when she remembers that grace has not been said. Mechanically she folds her hands without, however, managing to suppress her meanness.)*

MRS. SPILLER. *(Intoning.)*

> Come, Lord Jesus, be our guest.
> May thy bounty to us be blessed.
> A-men.

They take their seats noisily. With all the passing and taking of the many dishes, which occupies no mean amount of time, they manage to get over the awkwardness of the previous interchange.

HOFFMANN. *(To Loth.)* Help yourself, Alfred. How about some oysters?

LOTH. I'll give them a try. First time for me.

MRS. KRAUSE. *(Who has just slurped one down noisily and speaks with freshly restuffed mouth.)* Ya mean this season?

LOTH. I mean ever.

Mrs. Krause and Mrs. Spiller exchange glances.

HOFFMANN. *(To Kahl, who is squeezing the juice from a lemon with his teeth.)* Haven't seen you for two days, Mr. Kahl. Been busy shooting up the fieldmice?

KAHL. Aw, g-g-go on.

HOFFMANN. *(To Loth.)* You see, Mr. Kahl is passionately devoted to hunting.

KAHL. F-f-fieldmice is inf-f-famous amph-ph-phibians!

HELEN. *(Bursts out laughing.)* That's just too absurd. Wild or domestic, tame or game, he can't see anything that moves without shooting it!

KAHL. L-las' night, I g-g-gunned down our ol' s-s-sow.

LOTH. Seems that shooting is your primary occupation.

MRS. KRAUSE. Mr. Kahl does it strickly fer 'is personal pleasure.

MRS. SPILLER. "Woods, wildlife, and women,"—as his Excellency, Minister von Schadendorf, used to say.

KAHL. 'N d-day after t-t-t'morrow, we're g-gonna have a pigeon shoot.

LOTH. What in the world is that supposed to be: a pigeon shoot?

HELEN. I simply can't bear that sort of thing. It's just sadistic and childish. A boy who pitches a stone through a window is doing something more constructive.

HOFFMANN. Isn't that a bit much, Helen?

HELEN. I'm not sure. From my point of view, it makes a lot more sense to smash windows than to tie pigeons to a post and then try to shoot them.

HOFFMANN. But, Helen, you really must consider...

LOTH. *(While cutting up something or other on his plate.)* It is a disgraceful barbarity.

KAHL. A c-couple o' lousy p-pigeons?

MRS. SPILLER. Nnngg—You know, Mr. Kahl keeps—nnngg—two hundred of them in his loft.

LOTH. All hunting is a form of the barbaric.

HOFFMANN. But one you can't exterminate. Right now, for instance, they're trying to track down five hundred live foxes, and foresters all over Germany are devoting their entire attention to looking into holes in the ground.

LOTH. Who needs all those foxes?

HOFFMANN. The English—who bestow upon them the honor of being released from their cages only to be chased to death by members of the aristocracy.

LOTH. Moslem or Christian—all the same. Once a beast, always a beast.

HOFFMANN. May I pass you some lobster, Mother?

MRS. KRAUSE. Sure. They're mighty tasty this year.

MRS. SPILLER. Madame has such refined taste—nnngg.

MRS. KRAUSE. *(To Loth.)* Guess ya never et no lobster neither, hunh Doctor?

LOTH. Yes, once in a while—by the sea up in Warnemünde,[8] where I was born.

MRS. KRAUSE. *(To Kahl.)* 'Times, honest-ta-God, a body don't know *what* to eat no more, hunh William?

KAHL. D-d-damn right, c-cousin!

EDWARD. *(About to pour champagne into Loth's glass.)* Champagne, sir?

LOTH. *(Quickly covers his glass with his hand.)* No! . . . No, thank you.

HOFFMANN. Don't be silly.

HELEN. What? You don't drink?

LOTH. No, Miss Krause.

---

8. A port on the Baltic Sea, Warnemünde is now in the German Democratic Republic (East Germany).

HOFFMANN. Now, look here, Alfred. . . . This is getting to be a bit of a bore, isn't it?
LOTH. Were I to drink, I'd only become a bigger bore.
HELEN. That's very interesting, Doctor.
LOTH. *(Tactlessly.)* What? That drinking wine makes me even more boring?
HELEN. *(Somewhat taken aback.)* No! Oh my, no—not that. Only that you don't drink. . . . I mean, not at all.
LOTH. Why should that be particularly interesting?
HELEN. *(Blushing.)* It's . . . it's just so unusual. *(She grows even more flushed and embarrassed.)*
LOTH. *(Heavy handed.)* Absolutely correct—unfortunately.
MRS. KRAUSE. *(To Loth.)* This stuff sets us back fifteen Marks a bottle. Ya don't gotta be scared t' drink it. Comes straight from Rheims. We ain't puttin' no cheap swill in front o' ya; wouldn' touch it ourselves.
MRS. SPILLER. Oh, believe me, Doctor—nnngg—if his Excellency, Minister von Schadendorf, had—nnngg—been able to set such a table . . .
KAHL. I couldn't live without my wine.
HELEN. *(To Loth.)* Could you tell us why you don't drink?
LOTH. With pleasure. I . . .
HOFFMANN. Oh, what is all this, Alfred? *(He takes the bottle from the servant so that he may now try to inflict it upon Loth.)* Think about the good old days, how we used to spend many a happy hour . . .
LOTH. No, please. Don't bother to . . .
HOFFMANN. Drink today—just this once.
LOTH. You're wasting your time.
HOFFMANN. For me!

Hoffmann tries to pour; Loth resists; a slight scuffling of hands.

LOTH. No. . . . No. . . . I mean it . . . No! . . . No, thank you.
HOFFMANN. Don't be offended now, but aren't you being downright difficult?
KAHL. *(To Mrs. Spiller.)* A man who don't want nothin' 's already got what he has comin'. *(Mrs. Spiller nods in resignation.)*
HOFFMANN. Thy will be done . . . but all I can tell you is this: without a glass of wine at dinner . . .
LOTH. And a glass of beer right after breakfast . . .
HOFFMANN. Well, why not? A glass of beer's a very healthy thing.
LOTH. And a little nip of cognac now and then . . .

Act I

HOFFMANN. You're not going to deny me *that* little bit of pleasure, are you? You'll never have much chance of turning me into an ascetic. What are you trying to do? Deprive life of everything that's stimulating?

LOTH. Not quite. I'm thoroughly satisfied with the normal stimuli that touch my nervous system.

HOFFMANN. Well, as far as I'm concerned, a group of people who sit down together and keep their throats dry enough to spit feathers is, and always will be, a hopelessly dreary and tedious lot, and one which, as a rule, I can do very well without.

MRS. KRAUSE. Even all them blue bloods drink like fish.

MRS. SPILLER. *(Solemnly confirming the remark with a stately bow.)* Drinking large quantities of wine—nnngg—is second nature to a real gentleman.

LOTH. *(To Hoffmann.)* My response is the diametrical opposite. I generally find myself bored to tears at tables devoted to heavy drinking.

HOFFMANN. Well, of course, these things must be done in moderation.

LOTH. What would you call moderation?

HOFFMANN. Oh . . . as long as you manage to retain control of your senses . . .

LOTH. Aha! Then you're willing to admit that the consumption of alcohol does indeed impair the senses. And that, you see, is why I find drinking parties such a bore.

HOFFMANN. Are you afraid of losing control of your senses all that easily?

KAHL. Th-th-th'other day I drank a b-bottle o' R-Rrrr-Rü-Rüdesheimer, 'n th-then one o' champagne. And on top o' that an-n-nother one o' B-B-Bordeaux, b-but I was n-n-nowheres n-near drunk.

LOTH. *(To Hoffmann.)* Of course I'm not afraid. You know very well that it was I who used to take you boys home after you'd had too much. And I've still got that same old iron constitution. No, that's not what scares me.

HOFFMANN. What then?

HELEN. Yes, what *is* your real reason for not drinking? Please tell us.

LOTH. *(To Hoffmann.)* All right, so that you'll be satisfied: I no longer drink, if for no other reason than that I have pledged by my word of honor to avoid all beverages containing alcoholic spirits.

HOFFMANN. In other words, you have cheerfully reduced yourself to the level of a temperance fanatic.

LOTH. I am a teetotaler.

HOFFMANN. And for how long, if one may ask, are you taking the pledge?
LOTH. For life.
HOFFMANN. *(Throws down his knife and fork and half rises from his chair.)* Jeee-sus! *(Plops down again.)* To be perfectly frank . . . I mean, I never thought you'd be so—if you'll pardon the expression—childish.
LOTH. You're welcome to call it that.
HOFFMANN. How in the world did you ever arrive at this sorry state?
HELEN. You must have rather substantial reasons.—At least, that's what I think.
LOTH. I do indeed have them. You probably have no notion, Miss Krause—nor do you, Hoffmann—of the horrible part that alcohol plays in modern life. . . . Read Bunge, if you want to begin to understand it.—I happen to remember what a man named Everett wrote concerning the significance of alcohol in the life of the United States.—*Nota bene*, his evidence covers a period of ten years. In that time, according to Everett, alcohol has directly devoured a sum of three billion dollars, and another six-hundred million indirectly. It has killed three-hundred thousand people; it has sent one-hundred thousand children into the streets to beg; it has driven countless other thousands of souls into the prisons and poorhouses; it has caused at least two thousand suicides; it is responsible for the loss of at least ten million dollars as a result of fire, violence, and vandalism; it has widowed no fewer than twenty thousand women, and it has made orphans of at least one million children. Worst of all, the effects of alcohol extend to the third and fourth generation.—Had I sworn never to marry, I might freely drink, but as things stand . . . After all, my ancestors were all healthy, vigorous and, as I happen to know, thoroughly temperate people. Every movement that I make, every hardship I surmount, every clear breath I draw makes me realize how much I owe them. And this, you see, is precisely the point: this heritage which is mine is one I am absolutely determined to transmit, both unsullied and undiminished, to any progeny I might sire.
MRS. KRAUSE. Hey—you know—them miners o' ours actually do drink too much. That's th' God's honest truth.
KAHL. Lap it up like a b-bunch o' p-p-pigs.
HELEN. Oh, my. You mean that such things are hereditary?
LOTH. Alcoholism runs in families. Some are destroyed by it.
KAHL. *(Half to Mrs. Krause, half to Helen.)* Your ol' man—he bends a hefty elbow, too.
HELEN. *(White as a sheet, furiously.)* Oh, stop babbling nonsense!!

MRS. KRAUSE. Will ya lissen to th' mouth on that female!! Y'd think she's a reg'lar princess. Playin' th' big society lady again, hunh?—That's th' way she shoots 'er mouth off to 'er future husband. *(To Loth, pointing to Kahl.)* That's what 'e is, ya know. It's all arranged.

HELEN. *(Jumping up.)* Stop it! . . . Just stop it, Mother . . . or else I'll . . .

MRS. KRAUSE. Well, if that don't beat all. Whadda ya say, Doctor? Ya call that eddication, hunh? I treat 'er like she was me own, but this is too much.

HOFFMANN. *(Trying to appease.)* Mother, please do me a favor . . .

MRS. KRAUSE. Not on y'r life! Why me? . . . A ninny like that! . . . There ain't no justice. . . . Ya dumb cow!

HOFFMANN. Mother, I must really beg of you to pull yourself togeth—

MRS. KRAUSE. *(With increasing fury.)* 'Stead o' such a female lendin' a hand on th' farm . . . oooh, no! God forbid! Jus' th' thought o' that makes 'er turn green. . . . Buuuut—ya take y'r Schillers 'n y'r Goethes, 'n all them stupid bastards who don't give ya nothin' but lies; thaaat gets to 'er—thaaat she likes. It's enough to drive ya crazy. *(She stops, trembling with rage.)*

HOFFMANN. *(Trying to placate.)* Easy, now—pretty soon she'll . . . well, maybe it wasn't quite right . . . maybe . . . it . . . *(Beckons to Helen who, in her excitement, has walked away. The girl, forcing back her tears, returns to her place. Interrupting the agonizing silence that has ensued, Hoffman speaks to Loth.)* Now, what was it we were talking about? . . . Oh, yes—our trusty old booze. *(He raises his glass.)* Well, Mother: peace be upon us! We'll drink a toast in peace, and pay homage to the old bottle by being peaceful. *(Mrs. Krause clinks glasses with him, albeit with marked reluctance. Hoffmann turns to Helen.)* What, Helen? Your glass is empty? . . . Will wonders never cease? . . . Loth, I do believe you've made a convert.

HELEN. Oh, no . . . I . . .

MRS. SPILLER. Oh, yes, Miss Helen. It surely looks as if . . .

HOFFMANN. Well, you certainly never used to be a prude.

HELEN. *(A bit haughty.)* I'm simply not in the mood today. That's all.

HOFFMANN. Well, I humbly beg your royal pardon, Madame.—Now, what were we talking about?

LOTH. We were discussing the fact that alcoholism runs in families.

HOFFMANN. *(Disconcerted again.)* Oh, Yes . . . yes, of course . . . but . . .

Increasing anger is noticeable in Mrs. Krause's behavior, while it becomes apparent that Kahl is making considerable effort to restrain his laughter about something that he finds dreadfully amusing. Helen is staring daggers at Kahl, and the clear threat of her glance seems repeatedly to be keeping him from saying something obviously on the tip of his tongue. Loth, calmly concentrating on peeling an apple, is oblivious to all of this.

LOTH. Seems also that you're blessed with more than your share of that sort of thing around here.
HOFFMANN. *(Close to having lost his composure completely.)* Why? . . . What . . . what do you mean, blessed? Blessed with what?
LOTH. With drunks, of course.
HOFFMANN. You really think so? . . . Oh, yes, sure . . . the miners.
LOTH. Not only the miners. Right here at the inn, for example, where I stopped off before coming to your house, there was a fellow sitting like this: *(He puts both elbows on the table, supports his head with his hands, and stares blankly down at the table.)*
HOFFMANN. Really? *(His embarrassment is now complete; Mrs. Krause coughs; Helen still has Kahl transfixed with her eyes. Kahl's whole body shakes with suppressed laughter, but he still manages to keep himself from bursting out.)*
LOTH. I'm surprised you don't know who this—you might call him "character"—is. After all, the inn is right next door. They told me he was a local farmowner—incredibly rich—who literally spends all his days and years swilling whiskey in this same tavern. Goes without saying that he's no more than a dumb animal today. He just stared at me with those vacant, besotted eyes of his. *(Kahl has been able to restrain himself thus far, but now he breaks out in raucous, loud, unbridled laughter, so that both Loth and Hoffmann stare at him dumbfounded.)*
KAHL. *(Stammering through the laughter.)* Honest-to-Ch-Christ, th-th-that's him. . . . 's g-gotta be . . . c-couldn' be n-n-nobody b-but the ol' man.
HELEN. *(Jumps up, shocked and infuriated. She crumples her napkin and hurls it down on the table. Bursts forth.)* You! . . . You are . . . *(Her loathing, unable to find words, expresses itself in the gesture of spitting at him. She exits quickly.)*
KAHL. *(Brusquely breaks off his momentary contrition resulting from an awareness that he has committed a massive blunder.)* Well, for cryin' out loud . . . of all the stupid g-g-goddam . . . I'm gettin' outa here! *(Slams his hat on, storms toward the door, and says, without turning back.)* 'Night all!
MRS. KRAUSE. *(Calls after him.)* Can't rightly blame ya neither, Will! *(Folds her napkin while calling.)* Miele!! *(Miele enters.)* Clear th' table! *(To herself, but audibly.)* Such a ninny!

HOFFMANN. *(Somewhat angry.)* Honestly, Mother, I must say . . .
MRS. KRAUSE. Oh, go to hell! *(Rises and exits quickly.)*
MRS. SPILLER. Madame—nnngg—has endured many a—nnngg—household nuisance today. So—nnngg—if you will kindly excuse me—nnngg. *(She rises and with eyes gazing upward, she offers a short, silent prayer before leaving.)*

Miele and Edward clear the table. Hoffmann has arisen and comes downstage with a toothpick in his mouth. Loth follows him.

HOFFMANN. Well, what can you do? That's the way women are.
LOTH. I have no idea what that was all about.
HOFFMANN. Isn't worth mentioning.—Happens in the best of families, as they say. And it shouldn't keep you from spending a few days with us.
LOTH. I'd very much like to have met your wife. How come we didn't get to see her?
HOFFMANN. *(Cutting off the end of a fresh cigar.)* Well, in her condition, you understand . . . women tend to be vain. . . . Come on, why don't we go for a walk in the garden?—Edward, serve coffee out in the arbor.
EDWARD. Very good, sir.

Hoffmann and Loth exit by way of the conservatory, R. Edward leaves by the middle door, upstage, and Miele, carrying a tray laden with dishes, follows him. The room is empty for a few seconds before Helen enters.

HELEN. *(Upset; her eyes tear-stained. She holds her handkerchief in front of her mouth. From the middle door, by which she has entered, she takes a few furtive steps to the left and listens at the door of Hoffmann's room)* Oh, don't go! *(Hearing nothing here, she hurries over to the conservatory door, where she also listens for a few moments, her expression tense. Then, with her hands folded, and in a desperately pleading voice.)* Don't go! Please, don't go!

Act II

It is about four in the morning. The lights are still shining through the windows of the inn. Through the gateway to the farmyard, we see the first signs of an ashen grey dawn which, during the course of the action, develops into a darkly reddish sky before gradually breaking into bright daylight. Under the arch of the gate, we discover BEIBST sharpening his scythe. He is about sixty. As the curtain rises, we see hardly more than his silhouette outlined against the grey morning sky, but hear the monotonous, uninterrupted, rhythmic clanging of the scythe hammer on the anvil. [9] *For several moments, it is all we hear. Then the solemnity of the morning's silence is shattered by the screaming clamor attendant upon the departure of the inn's patrons. The inn door slams shut with a crash. The lights go out. We hear the loud cacophony of crowing cocks and dogs barking in the distance. A dark figure, reeling and weaving its way toward the farmyard, becomes visible on the path leading from the inn to the house. It is old KRAUSE, who, as always, has been the last to leave.*

KRAUSE. *(Staggers against the fence, hangs on to it with both hands, and bellows back at the inn in a somewhat nasal and thoroughly drunken voice.)* Th' yard 'sh mine! . . . So's th' inn . . . 'Sh mine! . . . Horsh's ash of a barkeep! . . . Whoooo-heeee!! . . . Oh, boy. *(After grumbling and grousing something unintelligible, he frees himself from the fence and stumbles into the yard where he luckily manages to grab hold of the handles of a plough.)* An' thish farm'sh mine. *(Blabbers and half sings—the tune a barely recognizable rendition of "Trink, Trink, Brüderlein Trink.")* "Drink, drink . . . ol' brother o' mine . . . jus' leave y'r worries at—" . . . Brandy'sh good . . . gives ya couragsssh . . . Whooooo-haaaa! *(Bawling aloud.)* Hey! Ain't I a gor-geoush hunk o' man? . . . An' ain't I got a gor-geoush wife, hey? . . . An' ain't I got a couple o' gor-geoush girls?

HELEN. *(Comes quickly from the house. It is obvious that she has slipped into the first thing she could find.)* Papa! . . . Oh, Papa—come on in! *(She takes hold of him under one arm, tries to support him and lead him toward*

---

9. The conventional method of sharpening a scythe at the time of the play was to hammer the cutting edge of the blade until it was thin enough to be sharp.

Act II

the house.) Come *on*! . . . Please. . . . Quick . . . quick . . . come in . . . now!

KRAUSE. *(Has straightened up and tries to keep standing that way. Manages with both hands and considerable effort to extract a conspicuously swollen coin purse from his pants-pocket. In the slightly brightening light of morning, we see that Krause is dressed no better than the shabbiest of field hands. He is in his early fifties. He is bareheaded, and what sparse grey hair he has is uncombed and shaggy. His filthy shirt is unbuttoned to the navel. His leather breeches, tied at the ankles, were once yellowish but are now shiny with dirt; they are held up by a single embroidered suspender. His bare feet are stuffed into a pair of embroidered bedroom slippers whose needlework appears to be still quite new. He wears neither coat nor vest, and his shirtsleeves are unbuttoned. Finally having hauled out the purse, he holds it in his right hand and keeps dropping it over and over into the palm of his left hand, so that the coins jingle and clink. At the same time he ogles his daughter lasciviously.)* Hey-hey-hey!! The money-sh' all mine! How'd ya like a couple o' Marks?

HELEN. Oh, good God! *(She tries repeatedly, always in vain, to drag him with her. On one of her attempts, he embraces her with the clumsiness of a gorilla and tries to paw her obscenely. Helen utters suppressed cries for help.)* Let-me-go! I-mean-it! Let go this minute. . . . Oh, please, Papa! *(Starts to weep, then suddenly screams in extreme fear, loathing and rage:)* You animal! You pig! *(She shoves him away. Krause falls and lies sprawled on the ground. Beibst gets up and comes limping over from his seat under the gateway. Helen and Beibst try to lift him.)*

KRAUSE. *(Muttering in semisong.)* "Drink, drink . . . ol' brother o' mine . . ."

Now they have him up on his feet, and he stumbles into the house, dragging Beibst and Helen with him. The stage remains empty for just a moment. Noisy voices and door slammings can be heard from the house. A light comes on in one window, upon which Beibst emerges from the house. He strikes a match on his leather breeches and lights the short pipe that seldom seems to leave his mouth. While Beibst is thus engaged, Kahl is seen sneaking out of the house. He is in his stocking feet; his jacket is slung over his left arm; he carries his slippers in his left hand. His hat is in his other hand, and his collar is between his teeth. Having reached the middle of the yard, he turns around to find himself facing Beibst. For a moment, Kahl seems undecided. Then he manages to transfer hat and collar also to his left hand, reaches into his pocket with his freshly freed hand, and, coming over to Beibst, presses something into his hand.

KAHL. There's a M-Mark for ya . . . but m-m-mind ya k-keep y'r yap shut! *(He hurries across the yard, climbs over the picket fence to his house, L., and disappears.)*

Beibst has lit his pipe with a fresh match, limps back to his spot under the arch, sits, and gets back to the business of sharpening his scythe. Again, for several moments, we hear nothing but the monotonous clanging of the hammer and the old man's groaning, which he interrupts with short curses when something in his work displeases him. The morning has grown considerably lighter.

LOTH. *(Steps out of the house, stands still, stretches, takes a few deep breaths.)* Aaaah! Morning air. Nothing like it. *(Walks slowly upstage until he reaches the gateway. To Beibst.)* Good morning! Up so early?
BEIBST. *(Squinting up at Loth. Suspicious, surly.)* Mornin'. *(Short pause. Ignoring Loth, Beibst engages his scythe in conversation, addressing it with irritation as he swings it back and forth.)* Ya bent ol' piece o' junk! Well, ya gonna do the job? Ecchhh! Still no goddam good! *(Back to his sharpening.)*
LOTH. *(Who has seated himself between the handles of a cultivator.)* I guess you'll be harvesting hay today.
BEIBST. *(Gruffly.)* What kind o' jackass cuts hay this time o' year?
LOTH. Then why are you sharpening your scythe?
BEIBST. *(To the scythe.)* Ecchhh! Stupid piece o' tin.

Brief silence.

LOTH. Won't you tell me why you *are* sharpening it if it's the wrong time for harvesting hay?
BEIBST. Don't ya think ya need a scythe for cuttin' fodder?
LOTH. So *that's* what you're doing.
BEIBST. Well, what else?
LOTH. Do you cut it fresh every morning?
BEIBST. Well, d'ya want the critters to starve?
LOTH. You'll have to show a little patience and understanding. I'm ignorant city folk, you know; we're not all that well informed about the ways of the farm.
BEIBST. City folk! Ecchhh!!—Every one of 'em I ever met allus thought he knew all there is to know better'n us.
LOTH. Well—I, for one, don't. Can you explain, for example, what this implement is for? I think I may have seen one before, but its name escapes . . .
BEIBST. That there thing y're sittin' on? They calls that a cullervator.

LOTH. Oh, yes—a cultivator. You use one of those here?
BEIBST. Naw, sorry to say. He's let the whole place go to the dogs. . . . Th' whole farm. Jus' lets it rot, th' boss does. Many's th' poor slob'd like to get hisself jus' a li'l piece o' this land. Ya can't grow no grain in y'r beard, y'know. But not him! He'd sooner see it all go to rot 'n ruin. Ain't nothin' grows here but quack grass 'n weeds.
LOTH. But the cultivator would dig those out, too. I know that the Icarians already had them so they could till the land they had cleared.
BEIBST. Where're they from . . . them there I-car- . . . whatever ya call 'em?
LOTH. The Icarians? They're in America.
BEIBST. They got these here kind o' things already?
LOTH. Of course.
BEIBST. What kind o' people is them I-I-ca- . . . them whatchamacallits?
LOTH. The Icarians? They're not a distinct or specific race or from any one country at all, but a society of people from all nations who have united in a common cause. They own a sizeable parcel of land in America, and they farm it together. They share all the work equally—and all the profits, too. Not one of them is poor. There is no poverty among them.
BEIBST. *(His facial expression had been becoming a bit friendlier, but during Loth's last speech, it has reverted to its former suspicious and hostile look. Taking no further notice of Loth, he has totally refocussed his attention on his work with the prefatory words.)* Bent ol' piece o' junk of a scythe!
LOTH. *(Still seated, first looks at the old man with a quiet smile, then gazes out into the awakening morning sky. Through the gateway we now see wide expanses of clover fields and meadows. A brook, whose course is marked by alders and willows, meanders across the landscape. A single mountain peak breaks the line of the horizon. The larks have begun to sing all around, and the farmyard rings with their constant twittering, heard now from nearby, now from afar. Loth now rises and says.)* The morning is just too glorious. This calls for a walk. *(He exits through the gateway.)*—*The clatter of wooden clogs is heard. Someone is scurrying down the stairs leading from the stable loft. It is GUSTE [one of the maids].*
GUSTE. *(She is quite fat and is wearing only her underwear, leaving her neck, arms and calves bare. Wooden clogs are on her naked feet. She carries a lit lantern.)* Good mornin', Gramps.
BEIBST. *(Mutters something unintelligible.)*
GUSTE. *(Shielding her eyes with her hand, she looks through the gate after Loth.)* Who's the feller?
BEIBST. *(Irritated.)* Tries to make fools o' poor folk. . . . He can lie

worse'n any parson. . . . You jus' get a load o' his cock-and-bull stories sometime. *(He gets up.)* Better get the wheelbarrows ready, girl.
GUSTE. *(Who has been washing her calves at the well, is now finished. She speaks as she disappears into the stable.)* Right away, Gramps. Right away.
LOTH. *(Returns and gives Beibst a tip.)* Here's a little something for you. A man can always use a bit of money.
BEIBST. *(Suddenly transfigured into a sociable person. Sincerely good-natured.)* Oh, yes. Y'can bet on that . . . an' I thank ya right kindly.—I s'pose you're the son-in-law's company, ain'tcha? *(Suddenly very talkative.)* You know, if you're of a mind to go out walkin' toward that there hill, then ya best keep to th' left, all the way real close to th' left, you know, on account o' there's cracks in th' ground to th' right. Th' reason, sez m'son, he sez, is because they didn't board the place up right—the miners, he means. My son, he thinks them miners don't get nearly enough pay, so none of 'em gives a damn. Only kind o' work ya get down in them shafts is hit or miss, a lick 'n a promise, y'unnerstand? So, if you're headed that-a-way, 'member: stick to th' left; ain't nothin' but holes on t'other side. Was jus' last year when some butter-'n-egg lady, goin' along mindin' 'er own business, sank clean outa sight—right down into th' ground, God knows how many fathoms down. Ain't a soul knows where she ended up. So, like I sez, keep left, all the way left, if ya don't want no problems.

A shot rings out. Beibst, electrified, jumps up and limps a few steps into the open.

LOTH. Who's out shooting this early in the morning?
BEIBST. Who else? That no-good of a boy.
LOTH. What boy?
BEIBST. Willie Kahl—the neighbor's son. . . . Jus' you wait, you! I seen 'im. He guns down larks.
LOTH. Hey, you're limping.
BEIBST. Ain't that the meanest, the lowest o' th' low? *(Shakes his fist toward the field.)* Jus' you wait, you! Jus' you wait.
LOTH. What did you do to your leg?
BEIBST. Who? Me?
LOTH. Yes.
BEIBST. Somethin' musta gone wrong with it.
LOTH. Does it hurt?
BEIBST. *(Grabbing his leg.)* It's a tuggin', pullin' pain. Hurts like hell.

Act II

LOTH. Have you had a doctor look at it?
BEIBST. Doctors! Who needs 'em? Bunch o' simple apes—one's as bad as th' next . . . 'xceptin' our doctor here. Now there's a good man; knows what 'e's doin'.
LOTH. Was he able to help you?
BEIBST. Aaah, maybe a li'l bit over th' long haul. He worked my leg over a little. Squeezed it 'n poked it 'n punched it 'n twisted it some. But that ain't what I mean. He's . . . well, he's got heart. Got feelins f'r another poor guy's feelins. He'll buy ya y'r medicine himself. Don't charge ya nothin'. Come any time o' day or night. . . .
LOTH. But something must have happened to you sometime to cause that. You haven't always limped, have you?
BEIBST. 'Course not!
LOTH. I don't understand at all. There has to be a cause.
BEIBST. How should I know? *(Shakes a menacing fist once again.)* Jus' you wait, you . . . you with y'r bangin' away.
KAHL. *(Appears in his own garden. He holds his rifle barrel in his right hand; his left hand is closed. He calls over.)* Mornin' to ya, Doctor.

Loth walks directly across the yard toward him. In the meantime, Guste and another maidservant, LIESE, have each gotten their wheelbarrows on which there are rakes and pitchforks. They push the barrows past Beibst, through the gate, and out toward the fields. Beibst, after throwing a few furious glances and furtive gestures of rage toward Kahl, shoulders his scythe and limps after them. Beibst and the maids disappear.

LOTH. *(To Kahl.)* Good morning.
KAHL. Wanna s-s-see somethin' n-nice? *(He extends his closed hand across the fence.)*
LOTH. *(Coming closer.)* What have you got there?
KAHL. Guess! *(He opens his hand right away.)*
LOTH. Whaaat? So it's really true—you do shoot larks! You good-for-nothing lout! You ought to get a spanking for that kind of childish mischief. *(He turns sharply on Kahl and strides back across the yard and out the gateway, [momentarily] disappearing.)*
KAHL. *(Stares dumbfoundedly at Loth for several seconds, then shakes a clenched fist after him.)* Son of a bitch! *(Swings around and disappears, L.)*—*The yard remains empty for a few moments.*

Then Helen, in a light-colored summer dress and a broad-brimmed hat, enters from the house. She looks around, takes a few steps toward the gateway, stops and looks around again, before sauntering L. and turning into the path that leads toward the inn. Large packets of several varieties of tea leaves are slung across the fence to dry. She stops to inhale their aroma. Then she bends down a few lower branches of several fruit trees and admires their low-hanging, red-cheeked apples. When she notices Loth coming toward her, she becomes visibly even more restless, turns quickly and walks toward the center of the farmyard, arriving there even before Loth. Now she notices that the dovecote is still closed, and she goes toward it through a little gate that leads into the orchard. The cord that opens the dovecote has been blown about by the wind and has become tangled somewhere. While she is busy trying to pull it down, Loth has come over to the fence and speaks to her.

LOTH. Good morning, Miss Krause.
HELEN. Good morning. The wind's blown the cord up there, see?
LOTH. Let me help you. *(He also goes through the little gate, manages to get the cord down, and pulls it to open the dovecote. The pigeons fly out.)*
HELEN. Thank you so much.
LOTH. *(Has gone back through the gate again, stops, and leans against the fence. Helen is on the other side. After a short pause.)* Are you always up this early?
HELEN. I was just about to ask you the same thing.
LOTH. Who? Me? . . . Oh, no. It just seems to happen to me after the first night in a strange house.
HELEN. I wonder why.
LOTH. I've never tried to figure it out. Why bother? It wouldn't serve any purpose.
HELEN. Oh, why not?
LOTH. Well, at least no apparent purpose, and surely no practical one.
HELEN. So, everything you do or think has to serve some practical purpose.
LOTH. Precisely. And furthermore . . .
HELEN. I wouldn't have thought that of you.
LOTH. What, Miss Krause?
HELEN. That's exactly what my stepmother said the day before yesterday when she snatched *The Sorrows of Young Werther*[10] out of my hand.
LOTH. It's a silly book.
HELEN. Don't say that.
LOTH. I'll say it again. It is a book for weaklings.
HELEN. That . . . may well be.
LOTH. What leads you to this book, of all things? Do you understand it?

---

10. Goethe's *Die Leiden des jungen Werthers* (1774), a romantic novel whose hero commits suicide.

HELEN. I hope I do . . . partially, anyway. It soothes me to read it. *(Pause.)* If it really is as silly a book as you say, could you recommend anything better?
LOTH. Read . . . oh, let's see . . . do you know Dahn's *Struggle for Rome?*[11]
HELEN. No, but I'll be sure to buy it right away. Does it serve a practical purpose?
LOTH. Not really, but a rational and reasonable one. It depicts men not as they are, but as they should some day be. It is exemplary, sets us an ideal which we may emulate.
HELEN. *(With true conviction.)* Oh, that's admirable. *(Brief pause.)* Maybe you can enlighten me on another matter. The papers are full of talk about Zola and Ibsen. Are these writers really great artists?
LOTH. They are not artists at all, Miss Krause. They are necessary evils. I have a genuinely healthy thirst for art, and what I demand of an author is a clear, refreshing draught. I am not ill. What Zola and Ibsen offer me is medicine.
HELEN. *(Almost mechanically.)* Then maybe they have something for me.
LOTH. *(Who has gradually become more and more absorbed in his contemplation of the dewy orchard and has now given himself over to it completely.)* It's magnificent here. Look at that sun coming up over the mountain.—And all these apples in your garden—what a harvest.
HELEN. Three-quarters of them will be stolen again this year, as always. The poverty around here is simply too enormous.
LOTH. You can't imagine how deeply I love the country. Unfortunately, for the most part, my own crops must be harvested in the city. But for once I intend to enjoy a brief pastoral respite thoroughly. A man like myself needs a bit of fresh air and sunshine more than most people.
HELEN. *(Sighing.)* More so than others? . . . Why?
LOTH. Because I am in the midst of a gruelling struggle, the end of which I shall not live to see.
HELEN. Aren't the rest of us engaged in the same sort of struggle?
LOTH. No.

---

11. Felix Dahn's *Ein Kampf um Rom* (1876) was a popular historical novel of heroic deeds. Dahn, Professor of Jurisprudence at the University of Breslau at the time of the premiere of *Vor Sonnenaufgang,* extolled the virtues of the Romans and more particularly of the Goths. A pronounced attitude of national superiority permeates the novel. It was reprinted in the early 1930s and gained new popularity with the rise of the Nazis. There is now an inadvertent irony in Loth's high regard for this potboiler which glorified endeavors of conquest and self-denial in the national interest.

HELEN. But we're all involved in some sort of struggle, aren't we?
LOTH. Of course, but in one that has a chance of ending.
HELEN. Has a *chance*—there you're right. But why is there no such chance for *your* struggle, Mr. Loth?
LOTH. Because *your* struggle can, after all, only be one for your personal well-being. And an individual can attain this, insofar as is humanly possible. But *my* struggle is a pitched battle for the happiness of all mankind. For me to be happy, the entire rest of humanity must first be happy; I would have to be able to look around me everywhere and see neither disease nor poverty, neither servitude nor meanness. I could not, in a manner of speaking, take my seat at the feast of life except as the last of its guests.
HELEN. *(With deep conviction.)* Then you are a really, truly good man.
LOTH. *(A bit embarrassed.)* There's no particular virtue in my stance; it's no great moral choice; it's just my nature. Furthermore, I must admit that my struggle in the interest of human progress gives me great personal satisfaction. And this is a kind of happiness that I value much more than the sort that gratifies your run-of-the-mill egoist.
HELEN. I imagine that there are only a very few people who share your nature. It must be a joy to be born with it.
LOTH. Actually, one isn't really born with it. I think we are driven to it by the essential wrongness of the conditions that life imposes. But one must have deep feeling for that which is wrong—that's the crucial point. And when a man has that feeling and consciously suffers the wrongness of the human condition, it necessarily follows that he will become the sort of man that I am.
HELEN. Oh, if I only knew more. . . . What, for instance, would you call "wrong conditions"?
LOTH. All right! A few examples: It is wrong when the man who works in the sweat of his brow goes hungry while the indolent live in luxury. It is wrong to condemn murder in peacetime while we reward it in war. It is wrong to despise the executioner while we glorify the soldier brandishing his instruments of slaughter, strutting around with his rapier or his sabre at his side. Were that executioner to parade the same way with his axe, he would probably be stoned by an irate populace. And, finally, it is wrong to set up a state religion that calls itself the faith of Christ—a faith which teaches suffering, forgiveness and love—and then to train the people of entire nations to go out and butcher their fellow human beings in the name of that faith. And remember, these are only a few of the millions of examples of such madness. It takes no

mean amount of effort to come to grips with all of these horrid conditions. One must begin early in life.

HELEN. How did you ever manage to become aware of all this? It seems so simple, yet most people never give it a second thought.

LOTH. The way I grew up probably taught me what I had to know. That and conversations with friends, intensive reading, and a lot of independent thinking. I learned about the first of these wrongs when I was only a little boy. I once told a blatant lie, for which my father gave me a memorable hiding. Shortly thereafter, my father and I took a train ride together, and I discovered not only that my father also told lies, but that he considered it a matter of course to lie. I was five years old at that time, and my father told the conductor that I had not yet turned four. Children under four rode free of charge. Then I had a teacher who told us: work hard, be honest, and it shall follow as the night the day that you will prosper in this life. What that man taught us was not true; it didn't take me long to learn that. My father was a kind, honorable, honest, industrious, thoroughly solid citizen, and yet, a scoundrel who wallows in affluence to this day swindled him out of his last few thousand in savings. And my father, driven by need, had to take a menial job in a huge soap factory owned by this very scoundrel.

HELEN. People like myself hardly ever think of such things as major wrongs. At most we might feel that some injustice has been done, but we feel it only privately, and in silence. Come to think of it, I feel it quite often—and then a kind of despair takes hold of me.

LOTH. I remember one great wrong with particular clarity. I had always believed that there was no set of circumstances under which murder was not considered a crime, and punished as such. But after this incident, it became horribly clear to me that only the milder forms of murder are unlawful.

HELEN. How could that possibly . . . ?

LOTH. My father had worked his way up to foreman at the soap factory, and we lived right by the plant. Our windows overlooked the factory yard. I got to see a lot of things. There was a laborer who had been working at the factory for five years. He began to have violent coughing spells, and he kept getting thinner. I still remember when my father told us about him at dinner one night. He said, "Burmeister"—that was the worker's name—"Burmeister has TB, and it's going to kill him if he works in that soap factory much longer. His own doctor says so." The man had eight children. And weak and emaciated as he was, he hadn't any chance of finding work anywhere else. So he *had* to stay in the soap factory, and the boss even felt self-righteous for keeping him on—thought of himself as a philanthropist, exceedingly humane. One August afternoon—the heat was not to be believed—Burmeister was struggling with a wheelbarrow full of lime—trying to get it across the yard. I was just looking out the window. I saw him stop, then stop again, and finally keel over onto the cobblestones. I ran down to him. My father came. So did some other workers. You could hear the death rattle deep in his throat. His mouth was filled with blood. I helped carry him into the house. He was just a bundle of chalky rags that reeked of all kinds of chemicals. Before we'd even gotten him into the house, he was dead.

HELEN. How horrible!

LOTH. Hardly a week later, we pulled his wife out of the river into which the factory dumped its waste lye. And so, my dear Miss Krause, when a man is aware of all the things of which I am now aware, he can find neither rest nor peace, believe me. A simple little piece of soap that no one else in the world could think ill of, or even a pair of clean, well-cared-for hands are enough to depress me beyond endurance.

HELEN. I saw something like that once myself. It was horrible. God, it was horrible.

LOTH. What was it?

HELEN. The son of one of our workers was carried in here half-dead . . . about . . . three years ago.

LOTH. An accident?

HELEN. Yes. Over there in the big shaft.

LOTH. One of the miners, then?

HELEN. Of course. Most of the young men around here end up working in the pits. Another son of the same man also hauled coal down there. He was in a mine accident too.

LOTH. Both dead?

HELEN. Both dead. . . . Once it was an elevator cable that snapped. The other time it was a gas leak that caused an explosion. . . . Old Beibst has just his third son left, and he's been down to the mine since Easter time.

LOTH. How can it be possible? Doesn't the father have any objections?

HELEN. None. He's just even surlier than he used to be. Haven't you seen him yet?

LOTH. Should I have?

HELEN. He was sitting right by here this morning, under the gateway.

LOTH. You mean he's one of your farmhands?

HELEN. Has been for years.

Act II

LOTH. Does he limp?
HELEN. Very badly, as a matter of fact.
LOTH. Ah-haah! What happened to his leg?
HELEN. That's a ticklish subject. You've already met Mr. Kahl. . . . I'll have to come a bit closer to tell you this; I don't want anyone to hear. . . . You see, his father was just as fanatical about hunting as he is. Whenever the apprentices of the local craftsmen had to come out to the farm, he used to shoot at them, even if it was only into the air in order to scare them. He had a vicious temper too, especially when he'd been drinking. Well, I suppose that Beibst was grumbling one day—he likes to grumble, you know—so old farmer Kahl grabbed his rifle and let him have a barrelful. Beibst used to be the Kahls' coachman.
LOTH. Outrage upon outrage. That's all you hear.
HELEN. *(Growing more uncertain as she grows more excited.)* I've done a lot of thinking by myself around here. . . . There are times when I've felt so dreadfully sorry for all of them . . . for poor old Beibst and . . . The farmers are all so crude and so mean, like—well, like Streckmann. He lets his farmhands starve while he feeds his dogs fine pastry. Ever since I've come home from boarding school, I feel so out of place here. . . . You see, I've got my problems too.—But, I'm talking a lot of nonsense; it couldn't possibly be of any interest to you. You'd only laugh at me when I wasn't around.
LOTH. But, Miss Krause, how could you ever think that? Why should I?
HELEN. Well, why shouldn't you laugh? What you'll surely think is: she's no better than any of the rest of them.
LOTH. I think ill of no one.
HELEN. You'll never convince me of that.
LOTH. But what reason have I given you? . . .
HELEN. *(Close to tears.)* Oh, please don't talk any more. You *must* look down on us. How could you help looking down on us? *(Tearfully.)* Even my brother-in-law. Even me. Me above all. And . . . and God knows you have every reason to. *(Unable to control her emotions any longer, she quickly turns her back to Loth, runs out through the orchard and disappears. Loth passes through the little gate and follows her slowly.)*
MRS. KRAUSE. *(Comes out of the house. She is absurdly overdressed in her morning finery. Her face is livid with rage. She screams.)* Hey, you low-life slut! Marie! Ma-riieee!! Not under *my* roof, ya don't! You're on y'r way out o' here, woman! *(She runs across the yard and disappears into the stable. Mrs. Spiller, holding her crocheting, appears in the doorway. Sounds of scolding and weeping can be heard from the stable. Mrs. Krause storms out of the stable, driving the howling maid before her.)*

Out, ya scum, ya no-good whore, you! *(The maid howls even louder.)* Right now, this instant, ya get th' hell out o' here! Pack y'r few mis'rable rags 'n then *git*!

Helen, eyes red from crying, has come through the gateway. She stands quietly, watching and waiting.

MARIE. *(Discovers Mrs. Spiller and hurls down the milking stool and pail [she has been holding since coming from the stable]. Enraged, she starts for Mrs. Spiller.)* I got *you* to thank for this! I'll pay ya back, too! Jus' you wait 'n see! *(Sobbing, she runs up the stairs to the hayloft.)*
HELEN. *(Coming over to Mrs. Krause.)* What did she do?
MRS. KRAUSE. *(Gruffly.)* Any o' *your* business, ninny?
HELEN. *(Firmly, although almost weeping.)* Yes, as a matter of fact. It *is* my business.
MRS. SPILLER. *(Approaching quickly).* My dear Miss Helen, this is nothing fit for the ears of a young lady who . . .
MRS. KRAUSE. And why not, I'd like t'know, Spiller! She ain't made outa sugar. . . . She was in th' hay with th' hired hand all night, that's what. So now ya know.
HELEN. *(In a commanding voice.)* Nevertheless, the maid stays!
MRS. KRAUSE. Ya sassy skirt, ya!
HELEN. Very well! Then I'll tell father that you spend your nights in just the same way with William Kahl.
MRS. KRAUSE. *(Slaps her across the mouth.)* There's somethin' f'r ya t'think about instead!
HELEN. *(Deathly pale, but even more firmly.)* I said the maid stays! Otherwise, I'll tell the world—you and William Kahl—your own cousin . . . my fiancé. . . . I'll tell the whole world.
MRS. KRAUSE. *(Losing her composure.)* Who c'n say it 'n *prove* it?
HELEN. I can. This morning I saw him coming out of your bedroom. *(She exits quickly into the house.)*

Mrs. Krause totters, seems close to fainting. Mrs. Spiller hurries to her with smelling salts.

MRS. SPILLER. Madame! Oh, Madame!
MRS. KRAUSE. Sp-Spiller . . . the maid s-stays!

Act III

Time: a few minutes after the incident between Helen and her stepmother in the yard. The scene is that of the first act.

DR. SCHIMMELPFENNIG *sits at the table, downstage R. He is writing a prescription; his slouch hat, cotton gloves and cane are lying on the table before him. Short and squat, he wears a black suit-coat, has tight, curly black hair and a substantial moustache. His garb is altogether respectable, but not elegant. He strokes or twists his moustache habitually and almost without interruption. The more excited he gets, the more vigorously he tugs. He forces himself to maintain a look of calm composure while speaking to Hoffmann, but he cannot restrain a touch of sarcasm from creeping into the corners of his mouth. His gestures are animated, decisive and jerky, but seem thoroughly natural. Hoffmann, dressed in silk robe and slippers, paces back and forth. The table, upstage L., is set for breakfast: fine porcelain, pastry, decanter of rum, etc.*

HOFFMANN. Does my wife appear all right to you, doctor?
SCHIMMELPFENNIG. She looks well enough. Why not?
HOFFMANN. Do you think everything will go smoothly?
SCHIMMELPFENNIG. I hope so.
HOFFMANN. *(Hesitatingly, after a pause.)* Doctor, I decided—weeks ago already—to ask your advice about a very specific problem as soon as I arrived here.
SCHIMMELPFENNIG. *(Who has been answering while writing, puts down his pen, gets up, and hands Hoffmann the prescription.)* There you are! . . . I assume you'll have that filled immediately. *(While picking up his hat and gloves.)* Your wife complains of headaches. *(Looking into his hat; matter-of-fact, professional tone.)* Before I forget: see if you cannot somehow get your wife to comprehend that she is, to some degree, responsible for the new life about to arrive in this world. I've already had words with her about the consequences of lacing herself in too tightly.
HOFFMANN. Absolutely, doctor . . . I will absolutely do my best to impress upon her that . . .
SCHIMMELPFENNIG. *(Bowing a bit clumsily.)* Bid you good morning.

(Starts to leave, but stops again.) Oh, wait . . . you wanted to get my advice about something. *(Gives Hoffmann a cold look.)*

HOFFMANN. If you have a moment . . . *(Not without affectation.)* You do know about the horrible way in which my first boy died. You were right there. You also know how dreadfully it hit me.—One doesn't believe it then, but time really does heal. . . . When all's said and done, I even have reason to be grateful, now that it seems my fondest wish is about to be fulfilled. You understand that I must do everything . . . it's already cost me enough sleepless nights . . . and still I don't know how . . . simply do not know how to go about protecting this unborn soul from the monstrous fate of its poor brother. . . . And that's it . . . that's why I come to you for . . .

SCHIMMELPFENNIG. *(Dryly and businesslike.)* Separate the child from its mother: fundamental prerequisite for healthy development.

HOFFMANN. So, it *does* have to be that! . . . Total separation? Not even in the same house with her?

SCHIMMELPFENNIG. No, not if you're serious about your child's well-being. And, after all, your wealth allows you the freedom of this option.

HOFFMANN. Thank God it does. I've already bought a villa with a lot of ground around it near Hirschberg.[12] But I expected that my wife would . . .

SCHIMMELPFENNIG. *(Tugs at his moustache and stares at the floor. After reflecting.)* Buy yourself a villa someplace else for your wife.

HOFFMANN. *(Shrugs his shoulders.)*

SCHIMMELPFENNIG. *(Continues, as before.)* Couldn't you interest your sister-in-law in raising the child?

HOFFMANN. Oh, doctor, if you only knew how many obstacles . . . and, besides, she's young, inexperienced . . . just a girl herself . . . and a mother's *still* a mother.

SCHIMMELPFENNIG. I've given you my opinion. Good morning.

HOFFMANN. *(Excessively courteous, unctuously.)* And *I* bid *you* a good morning. I'm ever so grateful to you. . . . *(As both exit through the door, upstage C.)*

Helen enters. Her handkerchief pressed to her mouth, she is sobbing and distraught. She lets herself fall onto the sofa, downstage R. After a few moments, Hoffmann returns, newspapers in hand.

---

12. Hirschberg is the name of several towns as well as of sections in some larger German cities. Hoffmann is probably referring to the Hirschberg that lies in a quiet and picturesque locale near the highest elevations in Silesia.

Act III

HOFFMANN. What's this? Tell me, is this going to go on much longer? Ever since I've come here, not a day goes by on which I don't see you weeping.

HELEN. Oh, what do *you* know? If you had any sense of what goes on around here, you'd be even more surprised to see me when I *wasn't* crying.

HOFFMANN. This makes no sense to me.

HELEN. I know! Which is why it makes all the *more* sense to *me*.

HOFFMANN. So! Something happened again. Right?

HELEN. *(Jumps up; stamps her foot.)* Oh, for God's sake! . . . I can't stand it any more. . . . And it's going to stop! I'm not putting up with it any longer! I can't see why I . . . *(Her sobbing chokes her.)*

HOFFMANN. Will you, at least, tell me what this is all about, so that . . .

HELEN. *(Bursting forth with renewed fury.)* I just don't care anymore! How much worse can it get? I've got a drunk for a father, an animal—with whom his . . . his own daughter isn't safe.—An adulterous stepmother who wants to pawn me off on her own lover. . . . This entire existence altogether. . . . Oh, no—no one's going to force me to ruin my life and not expect to meet any resistance. . . . I'm leaving! I'll run away! And if you people won't let me go, then . . . a rope, a knife, a gun . . . all the same to me. Who cares? I don't want to start leaning on the brandy, like my sister.

HOFFMANN. *(Terrified, grabs her by the arm.)* Nellie! I'm telling you. Keep quiet! Not a word about that.

HELEN. I don't care! I don't care at all! I'm . . . I'm so ashamed . . . to the depths of my soul. I wanted to learn something, be someone, just have a chance. What do I have to show for it?

HOFFMANN. *(Who has not let go of her arm, begins gradually to force the girl over toward the sofa. In the tone of his voice, there is a sudden soft, exaggerated, almost vibrant tenderness.)* Nellie, I know only too well how much you have to endure around here. Easy, now. This is *me*, remember? You don't have to tell *me*. *(Placing his right hand caressingly on her shoulder, he brings his face close to hers.)* Believe me, I can't bear to see you crying. It hurts me. But, please don't make things out to be even drearier than they are. Don't forget, you and I . . . we two together . . . we're, in a way, in the same position. I've gotten myself into this . . . this peasant atmosphere. Do I belong here? Surely, it suits me as little as it does you.

HELEN. *(Still crying.)* If . . . if my poor, sweet little mother had had any way of knowing what was going to happen when . . . when she decided that I should be . . . be educated at Herrnhut. If only she'd let me stay at home, then I'd . . . I'd at least never have known that there's anything else. I'd have grown up blissfully ignorant in the corruption of this dump. . . . But now . . .

HOFFMANN. *(Has gently forced Helen down upon the sofa and sits beside her, pressed very close. His consolations betray an ever more obvious sensuality.)* Nellie! Look at me; forget all that; let me comfort you.—I don't need to tell you about your sister. *(Passionately and intimately, while embracing her more firmly.)* Oh, if she were only like you! . . . The way things are . . . tell me . . . what can she possibly mean to me? Nellie, is there another man anywhere—a cultured, educated man whose wife—*(more softly)*—is the victim of such a crushing compulsion? You don't even dare say it out loud: a woman—and brandy. . . . So, tell me, am I supposed to be any happier than you? . . . Just think of my little Freddie! Am I any better off? *(With increasing passion.)* So, you see, on the long run fate has been good to us anyhow. It brought us together. And we belong together. Our mutual sorrow has determined our mutual destiny—and that destiny is to be together. Isn't it, Nellie? *He puts his arms around her completely. She lets it happen, but her facial expression reveals that she has forced herself to acquiesce in passive endurance. She has become silent, quivering, tense with apprehension—as if she were awaiting a revelation, or the approach of something inevitable and inexorable.*

HOFFMANN. *(Tenderly.)* Why don't you follow my suggestion? Leave this house. Live with us. This baby that's coming needs a mother. Come and be that mother—*(passionately, deeply moved, sentimentally)*—or it won't have any mother at all. And then:— bring a little, just a tiny little, light into my life. Do it! . . . Do it! *(As he is about to lean his head upon her breast, she jumps up, incensed. Her expression projects contempt, surprise, disgust, hatred.)*

HELEN. Oh, you . . . you are . . . now I know what you're really like. Up to now, I've only been able to sense it, but now I know for sure.

HOFFMANN. *(Surprised, he loses his composure.)* What? . . . Helen . . . I can't make you out, honestly. . . .

HELEN. Yes, now I'm certain. You're no better than the rest of them. Not even by a hair's breadth. Better?? Worse!! That's what you are! The worst of the lot!

HOFFMANN. *(Gets up; with assumed coldness.)* Your behavior today is really quite peculiar, you know.

HELEN. *(Steps right up to him.)* You've got just one thing in mind, don't you? *(Half-whispering into his ear.)* But you use very different weapons from my father or my stepmother or my highly esteemed and honorable bridegroom—very different ones. Compared to you, they're all just little lambs. That has just now become crystal clear to me.

HOFFMANN. *(With feigned indignation.)* Helen! You're . . . you're out of your mind. This is plain and simple madness that . . . *(He interrupts himself and slaps his forehead.)* Oh, good God—yes, of course. It's obvious. . . . It may be a bit early in the day, Helen, but I'll bet you've already been talking to Alfred Loth this morning.

HELEN. And why not? By all rights, if we had any shred of decency left, he's the kind of man from whom we should be hiding in shame.

HOFFMANN. So, I'm right. . . . Aha! . . . That's the way it is. . . . Wouldn't you know it? And hardly a surprise to me at all. So, he took advantage of the opportunity to stab his benefactor in the back. Typical. Just what you ought to expect.

HELEN. As far as I'm concerned, that is really low.

HOFFMANN. I rather think so too.

HELEN. Not a word, *not one word* did he speak about you.

HOFFMANN. *(Evading the issue.)* If that's the way it is, then it is my duty—do you hear me? My duty—as a close relative to an innocent girl like you to—

HELEN. Innocent girl?! What has all this to do with anything?

HOFFMANN. *(Furious.)* Loth is in this house on my responsibility. All right, you'd better know the facts: he is—and I'm putting it mildly—an exceedingly dangerous fanatic—is our friend, Mr. Loth.

HELEN. Saying something like that about Mr. Loth sounds utterly ridiculous. It's laughable . . . absurd!

HOFFMANN. In fact, he is the sort of fanatic endowed with the gift for confusing the minds not only of women, but even of reasonable people.

HELEN. Yet another absurdity! After exchanging only a very few words with Mr. Loth, my thoughts became so exhilaratingly clear . . .

HOFFMANN. *(Tone of a reprimand.)* There is not a shred of absurdity in what I am telling you.

HELEN. You have to have a sense of the ridiculous in order to recognize the absurd, and you haven't got it.

HOFFMANN. *(Still censuring.)* That is not the point at issue. I repeat: I speak not absurdity, but rather that which I must implore you to accept as incontrovertibly true. I speak from experience. He manages to befog your mind for you, and all of a sudden you find yourself ranting about the universal brotherhood of man, about freedom, about equality. Then you start considering yourself above every tradition, every convention, every established ethic. Once upon a time, for the sake of this insanity, we were—God knows—prepared to trample on the corpses of our own parents to achieve our ends. And you can believe me when I tell you that he would, if need be, do the same thing to this very day.

HELEN. And how many parents manage each livelong day to march over the bodies of their children without anyone even . . .

HOFFMANN. *(Interrupting her.)* Nonsense! That takes the cake! . . . I'm telling you, beware of him. Beware—and I emphasize explicitly—in *every* respect. He hasn't the slightest tinge of moral scruples.

HELEN. Now you're making ridiculous noises again. Believe me, once you really pay some mind to these things . . . they're incredibly interesting.

HOFFMANN. Say and believe what you will. Whatever the case, I've warned you. Let me add just one thing in strictest confidence: I very nearly got into the same horrible mess he did—*with* him, and *because* of him. I saved myself by a hair.

HELEN. If he's all that dangerous, why were you so genuinely delighted yesterday, when he . . .

HOFFMANN. Good God, we were boyhood friends! . . . Besides, how do you know I didn't have very specific reasons for . . .

HELEN. Reasons? For what?

HOFFMANN. Never mind.—Nevertheless, were he to arrive *today*, with me knowing what I now know—

HELEN. And what, precisely, is it that you know? I've already told you that he didn't say a solitary word about you.

HOFFMANN. You can take my word for it. I'd have been very careful. I'd have thought about it more than once before deciding to let him stay here. Loth is, and always will be, a man with whom association is damaging and compromising. The authorities are keeping an eye on him.

HELEN. What for? Has he committed a crime?

HOFFMANN. The less said, the better. It suffices to say that to go around in today's world with opinions the like of his is considerably worse and, above all, far more dangerous than stealing—of this I assure you.

HELEN. I'll make a point of remembering that.—But listen: now that you've said what you have to say about Mr. Loth, don't bother to ask me anymore what I think of you. Do you hear me?

HOFFMANN. *(Cold and cynical.)* Do you really believe that what you think of me interests me all that much? *(He presses the bell.)* Besides, I hear him coming. *(Loth enters.)* So . . . did you sleep well, old friend?

LOTH. Well, but not long. Tell me: I saw a gentleman leaving the house a short while ago.
HOFFMANN. Probably the doctor. He was just here. Didn't I tell you about him? This strange mixture of callousness and sentimentality.

Helen negotiates with Edward, who has just entered. He leaves and returns shortly to serve tea and coffee.

LOTH. This mixture, as you call him, happens to bear a remarkable resemblance to an old friend of mine at the university. I could have sworn it was a fellow by the name of Schimmelpfennig.
HOFFMANN. *(Sitting down at the breakfast table.)* Absolutely right: Schimmelpfennig.
LOTH. What do you mean "absolutely right"?
HOFFMANN. His name actually is Schimmelpfennig.
LOTH. Who? The doctor here?
HOFFMANN. You said so yourself just now. Yes, the doctor.
LOTH. Now, isn't that truly remarkable! Then it must be he.
HOFFMANN. Well, there you are. Kindred souls manage to find each other in the most out-of-the-way places. . . . You don't mind if I begin, do you? We were just about to sit down for breakfast. Please, go on; sit down. You haven't already had breakfast elsewhere, have you?
LOTH. No.
HOFFMANN. Well then. What are we waiting for? *(While remaining seated, he pulls out a chair for Loth. Then speaking to Edward, who arrives with tea and coffee.)* Uh . . . will we be honored by the presence of my mother-in-law?
EDWARD. The madame will be having breakfast in her room with Mrs. Spiller.
HOFFMANN. Well, that's a new one.
HELEN. *(Arranging the dishes.)* Drop it! There's a good reason.
HOFFMANN. You don't say? . . . Loth, help yourself. . . . How about an egg? Some tea?
LOTH. I'd rather have a glass of milk, if I might.
HOFFMANN. With pleasure.
HELEN. Edward, have Miele get us some fresh milk.
HOFFMANN. *(Peels an egg.)* Milk?—Ugghh! That curdles my blood. *(Reaching for salt and pepper.)* Tell me, Loth. What actually brings you to this neck of the woods? I've completely forgotten to ask you.
LOTH. *(Buttering a roll.)* I'd like to study local conditions.
HOFFMANN. *(Glancing up.)* Really? . . . What sort of conditions?
LOTH. To be precise: I want to examine the state of the miners here.

HOFFMANN. Oh, that! Generally very good, believe me.

LOTH. You think so?—It would be nice to be able to believe that, wouldn't it? . . . Oh, before I forget—you'll have to help me in this matter. You could make a valuable contribution to economics, if you . . .

HOFFMANN. I? . . . Me? . . . How?

LOTH. Well, you have sole control of marketing rights for the local mines, don't you?

HOFFMAN. Yes! . . . But, so what?

LOTH. It'll be a simple matter for you to arrange permission for me to inspect the mines. That is to say: I'd like to go into the pits daily for at least a month so that I can get a fairly accurate picture of how things are run down there.

HOFFMANN. *(Casually.)* And then, I guess, you'll want to describe what you've seen, won't you?

LOTH. Certainly. My work will be essentially descriptive.

HOFFMANN. I'm really terribly sorry, but I have absolutely nothing to do with that phase of the operation.—But you just want to write about the miners themselves, right?

LOTH. That question reveals that you're no economist.

HOFFMANN. *(Whose vain arrogance is piqued.)* I beg your pardon! Surely you must know that . . . well, *why*? I don't see why that isn't a perfectly respectable question.—And, after all, it would be quite remarkable if . . . Well, a man can't know everything, can he?

LOTH. Relax, will you! The fact of the matter is simply this: if I am to make a thorough study of the local miners, it is mandatory that I examine very closely all those conditions that determine their situation.

HOFFMANN. More often than not, that kind of writing is full of the most fantastic exaggerations.

LOTH. I have every intention of remaining innocent of that charge.

HOFFMANN. That will be highly commendable (*Again, as several times before, he casts a quick and meaningful glance in the direction of Helen, who has been hanging on Loth's every word with naive reverence. Hoffmann continues vigorously.*) You know, it's remarkable how some things just happen to come to mind at the strangest times. The workings of the brain are really a fascinating puzzle.

LOTH. And what, exactly, has worked its way into your brain all of a sudden?

HOFFMANN. Something about you.—I was thinking about your fian—oh, well—it's probably quite tactless to speak of matters so sensitive and private in a young lady's presence.

HELEN. Then, maybe, I'd better . . .

Act III

LOTH. Please, Miss Krause . . . you may stay without any fear of embarrassment, at least as far as I'm concerned. For some time now, I've been aware of what he's driving at, and it's absolutely nothing to be upset about. *(To Hoffmann.)* My engagement, right?

HOFFMANN. Well, since you've said it yourself, yes.—I was, as a matter of fact, thinking about your engagement to Anna Faber.

LOTH. She broke it—quite understandably—when I was sent to prison.

HOFFMANN. That certainly wasn't very nice of your . . .

LOTH. At least it was honest! The letter in which she called it off revealed her true nature. Had she shown it to me sooner, she could have spared both of us a lot of grief.

HOFFMANN. And ever since, you haven't found anyone else on whom to lavish your affections?

LOTH. No.

HOFFMANN. Of course not! So: gave it all up as a bad business, right? Sworn off marriage. . . . Sworn off alcohol. . . . The works! Oh well, *chacun à son goût*.

LOTH. It is not my taste at all, but it may well be my destiny. As I recall, I have already told you that as far as marriage is concerned, I have renounced nothing. I fear only this: that there is no woman anywhere suited to my temperament.

HOFFMANN. That's a pretty sweeping statement, Loth.

LOTH. I mean it! It's quite possible that one becomes too picky as the years go by and relies less and less on healthy instinct, and I still believe that instinct is the best guarantee of a suitable choice.

HOFFMANN. *(Frivolously.)* Oh, it'll crop up again some day— *(Laughing.)*—I mean, that instinct.

LOTH. In the final analysis, what have I to offer a woman? I believe less and less that I have any right to expect a woman to settle for that minuscule part of me that does not belong to my life's work. And then, also, I fear the cares and responsibilities that having a family entails.

HOFFMANN. You fear *what*? . . . The cares of marriage? My God, man, don't you have a head and arms?

LOTH. Of course, as anyone can plainly see. But, as I have repeatedly tried to tell you, the bulk of my productive energy belongs to my work, and it always *will*. It doesn't belong to *me* any more. Furthermore, there would be other most unusual difficulties . . .

HOFFMANN. Hey, listen! Doesn't that sound like someone ringing a sanctus bell in the background?

LOTH. You take all this for empty bombast?

HOFFMANN. To tell you the truth, it does sound slightly hollow. After all, there are those among us who are not necessarily primitive savages even though we may be married. Some people seem to behave as if they'd cornered the market on all the good deeds that need to be done in this world.

LOTH. *(Agitatedly.)* Not at all!—Wouldn't occur to me in the slightest!—Your fortunate financial status is one of the reasons you have become sidetracked from your life's work.

HOFFMANN. *(Ironically.)* So, that would be another one of your requirements, huh?

LOTH. What requirements? What are you talking about?

HOFFMANN. I'm talking about this: if you're ever going to marry, you'd insist on marrying money.

LOTH. Absolutely.

HOFFMANN. And then—if I know you as I think I do—you'd come up with an endless string of additional stipulations.

LOTH. A list I have already made! For example, a potential wife must possess impeccable physical and mental health. That's a *conditio sine qua non*.

HOFFMANN. *(Laughing.)* Magnificent! So, I guess you'll require her to have a thorough medical examination and a sworn certificate of total health before committing yourself.—Holy mackarel!

LOTH. *(Dead earnest, as always.)* Do not forget that I also make the highest demands upon myself.

HOFFMANN. *(With ever increasing mirth.)* I know, I know, I know! . . . Remember when you made a thorough investigation of all the available technical literature on the subject of human love, so that you could determine with unerring accuracy whether what you were then feeling about some girl or other really *was* love? So, tell us a few more of your absolute requirements.

LOTH. My wife must, for example, be capable of renunciation.

HELEN. If . . . if . . . Oh, I don't know if I should say it, but . . . aren't women generally accustomed to renunciation?

LOTH. Oh, for God's sake. You keep misconstruing what I say. That's not what I mean by renunciation at all. I demand renunciation only insofar as . . . better yet, I would merely ask my wife freely and cheerfully to do without that part of me that belongs to my work. . . . No, no! As far as everything else is concerned, it is my wife who should always stipulate and demand—all that her sex has been forced to forfeit for these thousands of years.

HOFFMANN. Oh, no. Not that too? . . . Women's emancipation! . . . Honest to God! Now, that's an admirable new twist. Now you're on the right track. Alfred Loth, better known as the vest-pocket agitator! What kind of demands do you have in mind in this department? Or, better yet, exactly how emancipated must this wife of yours be? . . . Go on—it's really great fun listening to you hold forth. . . . What does she have to do? Smoke cigars? Wear trousers?

LOTH. Hardly. Nevertheless, I would insist she be above certain social conventions. For example, should she really be in love with me, she must not be afraid to say so first, without waiting for me.

HOFFMANN. *(Is finished with breakfast. Jumps up in half-serious, half-joking indignation.)* You know? That . . . that is an altogether *shameless* demand. And may I predict, right here and now, that you will wait around till the end of your days before that happens. My advice is to scratch that one.

HELEN. *(Finding her internal torment hard to control.)* Gentlemen, if you'll please excuse me now—the household has to be . . . [*To Hoffmann.*] You know: Mama is up in her room, and that means . . .

HOFFMANN. Don't let us keep you.

Helen bows and exits.

HOFFMANN. *(With case for matches in hand, he strides over to the buffet, upstage R., on which there is a cigar humidor.)* No doubt about it . . . you sure can get a man's dander up . . . a thoroughly dreary talent, believe me. *(Takes a cigar from the humidor; sits down on the sofa, downstage R. He snips off the tip and, during the following speech, holds the cigar in his left hand while pinching the severed tip between the fingers of his right.)* In spite of everything . . . this is all still amusing. What's more, you wouldn't believe how good it feels to spend a few days in the country like this, away from business affairs. If only today, this damnable . . . what time is it anyhow? Unfortunately, I have to go to a dinner in town today.—No way around it. It's a banquet I had to give. What can you do, when you're a business man? One hand washes the other. That's the way the mine officials do it around here.—Oh, well! There's still enough time to smoke a cigar in peace and quiet. *(He takes the cigar tip over to a cuspidor, returns to his seat on the sofa, and lights his cigar.)*

LOTH. *(Standing at the table, leafs through a deluxe edition.)* The Adventures of Count Sandor.[13]

---

13. *Die Abenteuer des Grafen Sandor* sounds like one of the many banal Gothic romances popular in Germany during the late nineteenth century and published in expensive editions. If there actually was a novel with this title, which is distinctly possible, no record of it or reference to an author remains. The only hope for positively identifying the book is for someone to stumble across a copy in some attic or antiquarian book shop.

HOFFMANN. That's the kind of garbage you'll find turning up at any farmhouse around here.
LOTH. *(While flipping the pages.)* How old is your sister-in-law?
HOFFMANN. Twenty-one last August.
LOTH. How's her health?
HOFFMANN. Don't really know.—Seems all right to me, though. Does she seem sickly to you?
LOTH. Actually she looks more troubled than ill.
HOFFMANN. Oh, well! Just think of the constant misery she has with her stepmother.
LOTH. She seems to be substantially excitable, too.
HOFFMANN. What do you expect in this kind of an environment? I'd like to see anyone who wouldn't be excitable under these conditions.
LOTH. She seems to be very energetic.
HOFFMANN. Mere stubbornness!
LOTH. Sensitive too, no?
HOFFMANN. Too much so, most of the time.
LOTH. If conditions here make her so miserable, why doesn't your sister-in-law live with *your* family?
HOFFMANN. Ask *her!*—I've offered her that often enough. Go figure out women! They've all got their quirks. *(Cigar in mouth, Hoffmann pulls out a notebook and adds a few entries.)* You won't hold it against me, will you, if I have to leave you to yourself afterwards?
LOTH. Not at all.
HOFFMANN. How long do you think you'll be . . .
LOTH. I intend to find a place of my own very soon. Where does Schimmelpfennig live? It might be best to see him. He ought to be able to arrange something for me. I hope the right thing turns up at once. Otherwise, I'll spend the night at the inn next door.
HOFFMANN. What for? You'll stay with us till tomorrow, that's certain. Of course, I'm only a guest in this house myself—otherwise, naturally, I'd ask you to . . . you *do* understand!
LOTH. Perfectly.
HOFFMANN. But say—were you really being serious?
LOTH. You mean about spending tonight at the inn?
HOFFMANN. Nonsense! Absolutely not! I mean what you were talking about before—all this business about some twisted expository article you've got in mind.
LOTH. Why not?
HOFFMANN. To tell you the truth, I thought you were joking. *(Rises; speaks in confidential tones which seem half in jest.)* Come, now. Are you really capable of undermining the ground *here*, of all places,

Act III 53

where a friend of yours has had the good fortune to get a solid foothold?
LOTH. Word of honor, Hoffmann! I hadn't the slightest idea you were here. Had I known that . . .
HOFFMANN. *(Jumps up, overjoyed.)* Well, all *right*, then! If that's the way it is . . . look here, I can't tell you how happy it makes me to know that I wasn't wrong about you. Well, now you do know I'm here, and it goes without saying that I'll be glad to make up your traveling expenses and all the incidentals. And don't refuse out of politeness! It's simply my duty as an old friend. . . . That's the trusty old Loth I always knew. Just think of it: for a while there, I was seriously suspicious of you. But now I have to tell you in all honesty, I'm not nearly as rotten as I sometimes pretend to be. I've always thought the world of you—you and your honest, purposeful aspirations. And I'd be the last man not to be sensitive to certain of those unfortunately justified demands of the exploited, oppressed masses.—Go ahead, smile. I'll even go so far as to admit that there's only one party in parliament that has any real ideals at all—and that's the one to which you belong. Only—as I've said—slowly, man! Slowly!—Don't rock the boat. It'll all come, as it should, in good time. . . . Just a little patience! Patience!
LOTH. No question, one must have patience. But that doesn't give anyone the right to fold his hands and do nothing.
HOFFMANN. Exactly my opinion!—You know, in general, my thoughts have far more often agreed with you than my words. A bad habit of mine, I'll admit. I fell into it during too many dealings with people to whom I don't care to tip my hand. . . . On the subject of how to wive it properly, you also had a number of things to say that were right on target. *(In the meantime he has gone to the telephone, cranks it, and speaks alternately into the phone and to Loth.)* By the way, my little sister-in-law was all ears. . . . *(Into phone.)* Franz! Have the carriage ready in ten minutes. . . . *(To Loth.)* They made quite an impression on her. . . . *(Into phone.)* What?—Nonsense!—Well, that beats everything. . . . Then hitch up the black horses immediately. . . . *(To Loth.)* And why shouldn't they have impressed her, after all? . . . *(Into phone.)* Jesus Christ on a crutch! To the milliner, you say? The madame went . . . the ma—Well, all right then! But right *now*! . . . Yes! Yes, of course! . . . All right! . . . That's it! I'm hanging up! *(Does so, then pushes buzzer for servant. To Loth.)* Just you wait, you! Just give me a chance to pile up the requisite mountain of shekels, and then we'll see what happens around here. *(Edward has entered.)* Edward! Boots with spats and

my walking coat! *(Edward exits.)* I may just decide to do something that'll surprise every one of you. . . . If, in about two or three days—you're absolutely going to have to stay with us till then—I'd have to take it as a real personal insult if you didn't—*(He takes off his robe.)*—All right then, in two or three days, when you're ready to leave, I'll drive you over to the train with my carriage. *(Edward enters, bringing coat and boots. Hoffmann allows himself to be helped on with the coat.)* So! *(Sits down on a chair.)* Now, the boots! *(After having pulled on one of them.)* That's one!

LOTH. Apparently you haven't quite understood what I was saying.

HOFFMANN. Oh, well. That's distinctly possible. You lose track of things, you know. Nothing but the daily grind of business around here. . . . Edward, hasn't the mail come yet today? Wait a minute!—Go into my room, will you. On the left side of my desk you'll find a document with a blue cover. Go get it and bring it out to the carriage. *(Edward exits to Hoffmann's room, L., returns with folder, then goes out center door, upstage.)*

LOTH. I merely mean that you didn't understand me in one respect.

HOFFMANN. *(Still agonizing over the second boot.)* Uh-u-u-h! . . . Aaaah! So! *(Stands up and stamps each foot securely into its boot.)* There we are! Nothing's more annoying than tight boots. . . . Now, what were you just saying?

LOTH. You spoke of my departure. . . .

HOFFMANN. So?

LOTH. I thought I had told you quite emphatically that I intended to stay in this town for a very specific purpose.

HOFFMANN. *(Thoroughly taken aback and enraged at the same time.)* Now, you listen to me! . . . That comes close to rottenness. Don't you have any idea what you owe me as a friend?

LOTH. Well, surely not the betrayal of my principles!

HOFFMANN. *(Beside himself.)* If that's the way it's going to be, then I haven't the slightest reason for dealing with *you* as a friend. Let me tell you—and I'm putting it mildly, friend—that as far as I'm concerned, you've got your gall coming around here with that kind of behavior.

LOTH. *(Very calmly.)* Perhaps you'll explain to me what gives you the right to hurl such epithets . . .

HOFFMANN. Don't tell me you need *that* explained too! You are really the end! To be that insensitive you've got to have a rhino's hide rather than skin on your back. You march in here, enjoy my hospitality, toss around a couple of your worn-out slogans, turn my sister-in-law's head, give me a bunch of twaddle about old friendship and so forth, and then you stand there with a straight

Act III

face and tell me that you're going to write an essay delineating local conditions. What do you take me for, anyway? Do you think I don't know that your kind of so-called essays are nothing but shameless, muckraking lies? That's what you intend to write about our coal district, isn't it? A bunch of slander! Can't you see who'd suffer the worst injuries from your libelous distortions? Me! Only me! Corrupters of the body politic like you ought to be stomped on even more firmly than you are! Have you any idea what you're doing? You make the miners dissatisfied and demanding; you get them all worked up, make them bitter, rebellious, recalcitrant, downright unhappy! Promise them pie in the sky while you're picking their pockets of the few miserable pennies that stand between them and starvation!

LOTH. Now, do you finally consider yourself unmasked?

HOFFMANN. *(Brutally.)* Oh, go on, you ridiculous, pompous blowhard! Do you really think I care one jot about being unmasked by the likes of you?—Why don't you get a job instead? Stop all this crazy drivel!—*Do* something! *Get* somewhere! *I* don't have to crawl to anyone to mooch 200 marks. *(Exits sharply through the middle door, upstage.)*

For a few moments, Loth looks calmly after him. Then, no less calmly, he pulls his wallet from his breast pocket and removes a slip of paper—Hoffmann's check—and tears it into several pieces. He drops the scraps slowly into the coal bin. Then he takes his hat and cane and turns to leave. Helen appears at the conservatory threshold.

HELEN. *(Softly)* Mr. Loth!

LOTH. *(Startled, he turns.)* Oh, it's you. . . . Well, at least I can bid *you* farewell.

HELEN. *(Unintentionally.)* Because you feel that you *need* to?

LOTH. Yes! I do feel that need. . . . Since you were in there, I imagine you overheard the little scene in here, and so . . .

HELEN. I heard it all.

LOTH. Well, then—it shouldn't come as any surprise to you that I'm leaving this house without a flourish of trumpets.

HELEN. N—no! . . . I understand. . . . But maybe you could bring yourself not to be too angry with him. My brother-in-law is always quick to regret what he says and does. I've often . . .

LOTH. Could be. But that's the very reason I have for believing that what he just said is his real opinion of me. As a matter of fact, I'm certain that it is.

HELEN. You don't seriously believe that, do you?

LOTH. Oh, yes I do—and quite seriously. And so . . *He walks toward her and takes her hand.)* I wish you the very best of everything . . . always. *(He turns to leave, but suddenly stops.)* I don't know! . . . That is, rather: *(looking Helen calmly and directly in the face)* I know . . . really know . . . though I didn't till this very minute . . . that it isn't altogether easy for me to go away from here . . . and . . . that is to say . . . well . . . yes, that's it!

HELEN. If I were to beg you—really beg you—to remain a while longer—

LOTH. In other words, you do not share your brother-in-law's opinion?

HELEN. No!—And that's what I wanted to . . . absolutely had to tell you yet before . . . before you went.

LOTH. *(Grasps her hand once again.)* That makes me very happy.

HELEN. *(Fighting with herself. Her excitement increases rapidly to the point where she is in peril of losing consciousness. With monumental effort, she stammers it out.)* And more . . . there's even more that I wanted to . . . to tell you. . . . That . . . that is . . . that I . . . admire you . . . and . . . respect you—respect you as I've never respected any man before . . . and that I . . . believe in you and confide to you that . . . I'm ready to prove that . . . that I have . . . very deep feelings . . . toward you. *(She sinks into his arms in a faint.)*

LOTH. Helen!

Act IV

The farmyard, as in Act II. Time: fifteen minutes after Helen's declaration of love.

With considerable effort, Marie and GOLISCH the cowherd are lugging a wooden chest down the stairs from the loft. Loth, dressed for departure, comes from the house and walks slowly and thoughtfully across the yard. Just before he turns into the path leading to the inn, he finds himself facing Hoffmann, who has come toward Loth through the main entrance in a substantial hurry.

HOFFMANN. *(Top hat, kid gloves.)* Don't be angry with me. *(He bars Loth's pathway and seizes both of his hands.)* I take it all back! . . . Tell me how I can make it up to you. . . . Name any way at all, and I'm ready to do it! . . . I really regret all that. I'm deeply sorry.
LOTH. That doesn't help either of us very much.
HOFFMANN. Oh, please—if you're really . . . Look! . . . There isn't any more a man can actually do, is there?—Believe me, my conscience simply refused to stop hounding me. Just before I got to Jauer, I turned back. . . . That should make you realize that this means a lot to me. . . . Where were you going?
LOTH. To the inn—for the time being.
HOFFMANN. You can't do that to me! . . . You just can't do that to me! Believe me, I realize that I must have hurt you deeply, and it'll probably take more than a few words to patch it up. Only don't deprive me of every opportunity . . . every possibility to prove to you . . . Are you listening? Come back! . . . Stay at least . . . at least till tomorrow. Or till . . . till I return. I have to talk all this over with you leisurely. You can't deny me that.
LOTH. If it means all that much to you . . .
HOFFMANN. It does! . . . Everything! . . . I swear! . . . Everything! . . . Come on, then . . . please! Don't run out on me now! *(He leads Loth, who no longer resists, back toward the house, into which both exit.)*

In the meantime, the fired maid and the young cowherd have hauled the chest onto a wheelbarrow. Golisch has rolled up his leather carrying strap.

MARIE. *(While pressing something into Golisch's hand.)* Here y'are, Golie! Have a li'l somethin'.
GOLISCH. *(Refuses it.)* Naaaaa! Keep it y'rself!
MARIE. G'wan, ya stupe!
GOLISCH. Guess I might as well. *(He takes the coin and puts it in his leather purse.)*
MRS. SPILLER. *(Yells out from one of the windows of the house.)* Marie!
MARIE. Whaddaya want now?
MRS. SPILLER. *(Emerging from the door after a moment.)* The madame's decided to keep you. All you have to do is promise . . .
MARIE. A stinkin' lot o' nothin' I'll promise her!—Get goin', Golie!
MRS. SPILLER. *(Coming closer.)* The madame would also like to— nnngg—add a little to your wages, if you . . . *(Suddenly whispering.)* Don't make an issue out of it, girl! She just—nnngg—kind of flies off the handle once in a while.
MARIE. *(Furiously.)* Let 'er keep 'er lousy couple o' pennies! *(Whining.)* I'd sooner starve! *(She follows Golisch, who has already started off with the wheelbarrow.)* Naaa—of all th' . . . on top o' everythin' else . . . 'ts enough t'make ya . . . *(She is gone. Mrs. Spiller follows her.)*

BAER, *known as "Hoppy Baer,"*[14] *comes in through the main gate. A stringbean of a man with a vulture's neck on which there is a perceptible goiter, he is barefoot and hatless. His raggedly frayed pants barely cover his knees. What little brown hair he has at the back and sides of his bald head is matted, dusty, and hangs down over his shoulders. He walks like an ostrich. Behind him, he pulls a toy wagon full of sand. His face is beardless. His entire appearance reveals that he is a seedy, shabby peasant boy in his twenties.*

BAER. *(With a strange, bleating voice.)* Saaa—aand! . . . I got saaa— aand!

He crosses the yard and disappears between the house and the stables. Hoffmann and Helen enter from the house. Helen is pale and carries an empty glass in her hand.

HOFFMANN. *(To Helen.)* Entertain him a little! You understand? Don't let him go. It's very important to me.—Such a vain, ambitious . . . gets insulted right away. . . . Well, good-bye!—You know, maybe I shouldn't go at all.—How's Martha doing?—I've

---

14. His family name means "bear" in German but also connotes "clumsy oaf." *Hopsla* or *hoppla* is not only a command to hop or jump but also an interjection used upon seeing someone stumble or telling him to "watch out!" In Hauptmann's text, he is referred to as *Hopslabaer*.

Act IV

got the strangest kind of feeling, almost as if soon . . . Oh, nonsense!—Good-bye! . . . I'm late. *(Calls.)* Franz! Drive the horses as hard as they'll go! *(Exits quickly through the main gate.)*

Helen goes to the pump, fills her glass, and empties it in a single draught. She drinks half a second glass, puts it down on the pump, and strolls around slowly, looking backwards through the gateway from time to time. Baer appears from between the house and stables and stops with his wagon in front of the door to the house where Miele takes some sand from him. In the meantime, Kahl has become visible behind his fence. He is conversing with Mrs. Spiller, who is on the Krause side of the fence on the path leading from the main entrance to the yard. Both are walking slowly along the fence while speaking.

MRS. SPILLER. *(Lamenting.)* Ah, yes—nnngg—Mr. Kahl! Many's the—nnngg—time I've thought of you when—nnngg—ever our lovely Miss Helen. . . . She is—nnngg—after all, in a manner of speaking—nnngg—engaged to you, and so—nnngg— . . . Well, in my time! . . .

KAHL. *(Climbs up on the bench under the oak, downstage L., and fastens a titmouse trap to the lowest branch.)* So, wh-wh-when's that ab-b-bomination of a d-doctor gonna be on his w-way, hunh?

MRS. SPILLER. Oh, Mr. Kahl! Not so—nnngg—very soon, I fear. . . . Oh my, Mr. Kahl, I—nnngg—may have come down a step or—nnngg—two in the world, but I still know—nnngg—in a manner of speaking—what good breeding is. In this respect, Mr. Kahl—nnngg—our gracious Miss Helen—has not been—nnngg—treating you properly. Oh, no—nnngg—not at all. And that's something that—nnngg—in a manner of speaking, no one could ever have said—nnngg—about me. My conscience in this respect—nnngg—is, in a manner of speaking, as—nnngg—pure as the driven snow.

Baer has wrapped up the sale of his sand and is on his way out of the yard. At this very moment, he passes Kahl.

KAHL. *(Discovers Baer and calls him.)* Hey there, Hoppy Baer! Give us a little hop! *(Baer takes an enormous leap. Kahl bellows out a huge horselaugh and shouts again.)* Hey there, Hoppy Baer! Give us another hop!

MRS. SPILLER. Well—nnngg—yes, Mr. Kahl. I'm—nnngg—telling you this for your own good—nnngg. You'd better watch out!

There's—nnngg—something brewing between our fine young lady and—nnngg—

KAHL. Once! J-j-just once I'd like t' t-turn my d-dogs loose on that so-son of a bitch.

MRS. SPILLER. *(In utmost secrecy.)* You don't know the half of what—nnngg—sort of an individual we're—nnngg—dealing with. Oh, I'm so dreadfully—nnngg—sorry for Miss Helen. I got it straight from the—nnngg—policeman's wife who got it—nnngg—straight from the precinct—I think. They say he's a really—nnngg—dangerous man. The woman said—nnngg—her husband is under strict orders—just think of it—nnngg—strict orders to—nnngg—keep an eye on him. *(Loth appears from the house and looks around.)* Look at that!—nnngg—Now he's going after her. . . . Oh, oh—nnngg—oh! Isn't that just the saddest thing y'ever saw?

KAHL. Just you wait! *(Exits.)*

Mrs. Spiller heads for the door to the house. She bows deeply to Loth as she passes him, then disappears into the house.
Loth exits slowly upstage through the gateway. THE COACHMAN'S WIFE, an emaciated woman ground down by worry and hunger, emerges from between the stables and the house. She carries a large pot hidden under her apron and sneaks toward the cow stable while looking anxiously in every direction. She exits into the stable. The two maids, each pushing a wheelbarrow heaped high with clover, enter through the gateway. Beibst, his scythe over his shoulder, his short little pipe in his mouth, follows them. Liese has wheeled her barrow to the right barn door, Auguste to the left; and both girls begin to lug heaping armfuls of clover into the stable.

LIESE. *(Coming back out empty-handed.)* Hey, Guste! Marie's gone.
AUGUSTE. 'Zat a fact?
LIESE. Go in 'n' ask th' coachman's ol' lady. She's jus' gettin' 'erself a couple o' drops o' milk.
BEIBST. *(Hangs his scythe on the wall.)* Ya better not let that Spiller woman find out.
AUGUSTE. Aw, Jesus, no! Never! Not on y'r life!
LIESE. Poor woman like that. Got 'erself eight young 'uns.
AUGUSTE. Eight li'l brats! 'N' *they* gotta eat too!
LIESE. They won' even give 'er a drop o' milk. That's about as mean as y'kin get.
AUGUSTE. Where's she milkin'?
LIESE. Way in th' back. Th' new cow—Venus!

BEIBST. *(Fills his pipe. Holding his tobacco pouch with his teeth, he mumbles.)* Marie's gone, y'say?
LIESE. F'r sure! Got caught in th' hay with th' stable boy.
BEIBST. *(Putting the tobacco pouch in his pocket.)* Everybody gets the urge sometimes—women too. *(Lights his pipe, then, while exiting through the gateway.)* I'm gonna get me a li'l breakfast.
THE COACHMAN'S WIFE. *(Carefully hiding the pot full of milk under her apron, she peeks out the stable door.)* Coast clear?
LIESE. Y'kin come now. Ain't nobody in sight. . . . C'mon! Y'better hurry!
THE COACHMAN'S WIFE. *(To the maids as she passes them.)* It's f'r th' li'lest one what's on gruel.
LIESE. *(Calling after her.)* Quick! Somebody's comin'! *(The coachman's wife exits between the house and the stables.)*
AUGUSTE. 'Ts only our young Miss.

The maids resume unloading their wheelbarrows, push them under the gateway after finishing, and then exit into the cow barn.
Loth and Helen come in through the gateway.

LOTH. Obnoxious character—this Kahl!—Insolent. And a sneak!
HELEN. Up front in the arbor, I think . . . *(They go through the small gate downstage of the house, through the little garden, and into the arbor, down R.)* This is my favorite place. No one ever bothers me here when I want to read a little.
LOTH. A lovely spot.—Really. *(Both sit down in the arbor, somewhat at a distance from each other. Silence. Then Loth speaks.)* Your hair is so very thick and beautiful.
HELEN. That's what my brother-in-law says too. He says he's never seen any like it—not even in the city. The braid at the top is as thick as my wrist. . . . When I let it down, it reaches all the way to my knees. Go ahead, touch it! Feels like silk, doesn't it?
LOTH. Exactly like silk. *(He trembles, bends down, and kisses her hair.)*
HELEN. *(Frightened.)* Oh, please don't! What if . . .
LOTH. Helen, were you serious about what you said before?
HELEN. Oh, I'm so ashamed. What have I done? I've just thrown myself at you. What must you take me for?
LOTH. *(Moves closer toward her and takes her hand in his.)* You mustn't give it a second thought.
HELEN. *(Sighing.)* Oh, if Sister Schmittgen only knew. . . . I can't even picture it.
LOTH. Who is Sister Schmittgen?

HELEN. One of my teachers at boarding school.
LOTH. How can you worry yourself about Sister Schmittgen?
HELEN. She was a very fine . . . *(She suddenly laughs heartily to herself.)*
LOTH. What's driving you to such laughter all of a sudden?
HELEN. *(Halfway between devotion and caprice.)* Oh, my . . . when she used to stand in the choir loft and sing . . . she was toothless except for one lonely long one in the front. You know that hymn that goes: "The trumpet shall sound"? It always came out: "The ssstrumpet shall sssound." It was just too funny. And all of us always went into gales of laughter when that "ssstrumpet" resounded throughout the chapel. *(She laughs uncontrollably, and Loth finds her mirth contagious. She seems so delightful to him right now that he cannot resist the opportunity to put his arm around her. Helen parries his move.)* Oh, please no! . . . I really did just simply throw myself at you.
LOTH. Oh, will you please stop saying such things.
HELEN. But it isn't my fault, you know. You have no one but yourself to blame. You were the one who had to demand that . . .

Once again, Loth puts his arm around her and draws her closer. At first she resists a bit. Then she gives in and looks with open rapture into Loth's face, which is obviously bathed in joy as he bends it toward her. Inadvertently, in the awkwardness born of her shyness, she kisses him on the mouth first. Both blush; then Loth returns her kiss—long, ardent, intense. The exchanging of kisses—silent and eloquent at the same time—becomes their only conversation for a while. Loth breaks the silence.

LOTH. Nellie, isn't it? They call you Nellie here, don't they?
HELEN. *(Kisses him.)* Call me something else . . . call me what pleases you most.
LOTH. Darling!

The game of exchanging kisses and adoring glances repeats itself.

HELEN. *(With Loth's arms firmly around her, she rests her head on his chest. With hazy, deliriously happy eyes, she looks up at him and whispers fervently.)* Oh, how wonderful. How very wonderful!
LOTH. To die with you—like this.
HELEN. *(Passionately.)* To live! . . . *(She pulls herself free of his embrace.)* Why to die *now*? . . . Now . . .
LOTH. You mustn't misconstrue that. Since forever, I've found myself drunk with the notion . . . particularly in moments of great joy . . . drunk with an intense consciousness of the knowledge that it is within my own power to . . . Do you understand what I mean?

Act IV

HELEN. That it's within your power to wish for death . . . and grasp it?
LOTH. *(Without a trace of sentimentality.)* Yes! And that's why the thought of dying holds no horrors for me at all. In fact, quite the contrary. It's like reaching out to a good old friend. You call him, and you know he'll be there when you want him or need him. It's a feeling that helps you to transcend all manner of things . . . things past—and even things to come. . . . *(Gazing at Helen's hand.)* Your hands are so very lovely. *(He caresses them.)*
HELEN. Oh, yes . . . that's nice.—Oh! *(She seeks and finds his embrace once again.)*
LOTH. I mean it, you know. I never really lived . . . not until now.
HELEN. Do you think I have? . . . I feel all giddy—with happiness. Good God, how could all this . . . I mean so all of a sudden . . .
LOTH. Yes, all of a sudden . . .
HELEN. Listen, this is the way it feels: my whole life like a single day; yesterday and today like a whole year. Doesn't it?
LOTH. I came here only yesterday?
HELEN. That's right!—And that's just it—naturally! . . . Oh, my. *You* don't even know it!
LOTH. Me too! Honestly, it feels like . . .
HELEN. It does, doesn't it?—Like a whole duly recorded 365-day year? *(Half leaping up.)* Wait! . . . Someone's coming . . . *(They move apart.)* Oh, who cares?! . . . It all makes me feel absolutely daring now. *(She remains seated, and with a glance encourages Loth to move closer, which he does immediately.)*
HELEN. *(In Loth's arms.)* Hey, tell me—what do we do first?
LOTH. Your stepmother, I imagine, would be of a mind to tell me to be on my way.
HELEN. Oh, my stepmother . . . that's not going to be . . . It's none of her business! I'll do as I please! . . . I mean, after all, I do have my share of my mother's estate.
LOTH. Just because of that, do you think . . .
HELEN. I'm of age; father will simply have to give it to me.
LOTH. You're not on the best of terms with—everyone here, are you? . . . Where has your father gone off to, anyway?
HELEN. Gone off? Haven't you . . . ? Oh, you haven't seen my father yet, have you?
LOTH. No. Hoffmann told me . . .
HELEN. Oh, yes! Yes, you did already see him once.
LOTH. Not that I know of. . . . Where would I have, darling?
HELEN. I . . . *(She bursts into tears.)* No, I can't . . . can't tell you . . . not yet. . . . It's too terribly awful!

LOTH. What's too terribly awful? Helen, tell me! Is there something wrong with your father?

HELEN. Oh, don't ask! Not now! Later!

LOTH. Anything you don't feel free to confide in me is something I will never ask you to reveal. . . . Look, as far as the money is concerned . . . if worse comes to worse . . . I don't exactly earn a fortune from the articles I write, but we could make ends meet.

HELEN. And I wouldn't sit back and do nothing either, would I? Still, the better part of valor . . . My inheritance is more than enough—and your work shouldn't have to . . . No, you just can't give that up, not under any circumstances—especially now! Now you must really be able to attack it . . . completely . . . unencumbered!

LOTH. *(Kissing her fervently.)* Oh, my superb darling!

HELEN. Do you really, really love me? Really?

LOTH. Really.

HELEN. Repeat, one hundred times: "Really"!

LOTH. Really. Really. And irrevocably.

HELEN. No fair cheating!

LOTH. One "irrevocably" counts for a hundred "reallys."

HELEN. It does? Maybe in Berlin!

LOTH. No, only in Witzdorf.

HELEN. Oh, you! . . . Look me straight in the eye and don't laugh.

LOTH. Gladly.

HELEN. Has there ever been any-one, any-where, not counting your first fiancée, whom you have lo—? You *are* laughing, you . . .

LOTH. Darling, let me tell you something in all seriousness. I feel it's my duty. . . . There is a substantial number of women with whom . . .

HELEN. *(With a quick and vigorous motion, she puts her hand over his mouth.)* For God's sake, not now! You can tell me all about that some day—later—much later. When we're old . . . and I say to you: "Now!" But not before! Agreed?

LOTH. Agreed! Your wish is my command.

HELEN. Right now, I'd rather hear something tender. . . . Pay attention and repeat after me:—

LOTH. What?

HELEN. I have always . . .

LOTH. I have always . . .

HELEN. . . . loved you and only you . . .

LOTH. . . . loved you and only you . . .

HELEN. . . . for as long as I have lived . . .

LOTH. . . . for as long as I have lived . . .

HELEN. . . . and will love only you all the days of my life.
LOTH. . . . and will love only you all the days of my life—and that is true as truly as I am an honest man.
HELEN. *(Joyfully.)* I didn't say that.
LOTH. But I did. *(Kisses.)*
HELEN. *(Hums very softly. The tune "Du, du liegst mir im Herzen.")*
LOTH. Now it's your turn to make your confession.
HELEN. Anything you wish.
LOTH. Confess! Am I the first?
HELEN. No.
LOTH. Who?
HELEN. *(Laughing playfully [and deftly imitating the man she names].)* Willy K-K-K-Kahl!
LOTH. *(Laughing.)* Who else?
HELEN. Nooo-body! There isn't anyone else—really. You'll have to believe me—there really isn't. Why should I lie about it?
LOTH. So—there *was* someone else?
HELEN. *(Intensely.)* Please, please, please—don't ask me about it now. *(Hides her face in her hands and cries, seemingly for no reason.)*
LOTH. Nellie . . . Nellie, listen! I'm not trying to cross-examine you.
HELEN. Later! . . . I'll tell you everything . . . but later.
LOTH. Darling, I can only reiterate . . .
HELEN. It was someone—I want you to know this—someone whom I . . . because . . . because among so many bad people, he seemed somehow not quite as bad. It's all so different now. *(Crying against Loth's neck. Violently.)* Oh, if only I never had to be away from you at all anymore! Nothing could make me happier than to leave here with you this instant.
LOTH. I imagine things get rather grim for you in this house.
HELEN. An understatement, to say the least! What goes on here is simply horrible . . . an animal existence. It would have been the death of me if you hadn't come along. It makes my skin crawl to think of it!
LOTH. Darling, I'm sure it would set your mind at ease if you told me everything openly and honestly.
HELEN. I know, but . . . I can't bring myself to do it. Not yet . . . at least, not now!—I'm afraid . . . really afraid.
LOTH. You went away to boarding school, didn't you?
HELEN. It was my mother's decision—on her deathbed.
LOTH. Was your sister also . . . ?
HELEN. No. She always stayed at home. . . . And so, when I returned four years ago, I found a father—who . . . a stepmother—who . . . a sister . . . Can't you figure out what I'm trying to say?

LOTH. Your stepmother's quarrelsome. Right? Maybe a bit on the jealous side?—And mean!
HELEN. And my father? . . .
LOTH. Well, most likely he dances to whatever tune she calls.—Does she tyrannize him?
HELEN. If it were nothing more than that! . . . No! . . . It's just too awful.—You'll never guess. . . . It was my father . . . it was my father whom you . . . whom you . . .
LOTH. Nellie, don't cry! . . . Look, now I almost have to insist—strenuously—that you tell me . . .
HELEN. No! I can't! I don't have the strength—not yet—to . . .
LOTH. But you're destroying yourself this way.
HELEN. I'm so ashamed—so unbelievably ashamed! You . . . you'll reject me; you won't want to have anything to do with me! . . . It's beyond belief! . . . It's disgusting!
LOTH. Nellie, if you think that is what I would do, then you don't really know me. Reject you? Refuse you? Do I really seem to be as brutal as all that?
HELEN. My brother-in-law said that you would—quite cold-bloodedly. . . . Oh, no, no, no you wouldn't! Would you?—You wouldn't just crush me and walk away? Don't do it! . . . I don't know—*what* would become of me—then.
LOTH. But this kind of talk is madness! I don't have any *reason* to reject you.
HELEN. But if there *were* one, you might?
LOTH. No! Absolutely not!
HELEN. Suppose you could *think* of a reason.
LOTH. No doubt about it. There could be reasons. But they have nothing to do with what is at issue here. They are not in question.
HELEN. What kind of reasons?
LOTH. I would have to reject only someone who would force me to betray myself, my values, and my ideals.
HELEN. I'd be the last to do that.—But I can't help having the feeling that . . .
LOTH. What feeling, darling?
HELEN. Oh, maybe it's just because I'm only a silly little girl.—There's nothing to me. I don't even know what it means to have—principles by which to live. That's terrible, isn't it? It's just that I love you so much! And you're so good and so grand—and so brilliant. I'm so afraid that sometime—when I say something stupid or do something foolish—you'll realize that this was all a big mistake . . . that I'm much too silly for you. . . . Because, you know, I really *am* as simple and as plain as an old shoe.

Act IV

LOTH. How do you expect me to respond to that? Listen, you're everything in the world to me. Everything. What more can I say?
HELEN. I *am*, when all's said and done, in the best of health. . . .
LOTH. Tell me, are your parents in good health?
HELEN. Yes, of course! That is, mother died of a fever in childbirth, but my father is still hale and hardy; in fact, he must have an iron constitution. But . . .
LOTH. There! You see?
HELEN. And what if my parents were not healthy?
LOTH. *(Kisses Helen.)* But they *are*, Nellie.
HELEN. But suppose they weren't.

Mrs. Krause throws open a window and yells into the yard.

MRS. KRAUSE. Hey, you girls! Hey, out there! Gii-iirls!
LIESE. *(Emerging from the cow barn.)* Yeah, missus?
MRS. KRAUSE. Go get ol' lady Müller! It's startin'!
LIESE. Whaaat? Ya mean Mrs. Müller th' midwife?
MRS. KRAUSE. Who else? Y'deef or somethin'? *(She slams the window shut. Liese runs back into the barn and gets a shawl which she puts over her head as she hurries out of the yard. Mrs. Spiller appears at the door to the house.)*
MRS. SPILLER. *(Calls.)* Miss Helen! . . . Miss Helen!
HELEN. I wonder what's the matter.
MRS. SPILLER. *(Coming closer to the arbor.)* Miss Helen!
HELEN. Of course; that's what it is! My sister! . . . You'd better go. Around that way! *(Loth exits quickly, downstage R. Helen steps out of the arbor.)*
MRS. SPILLER. Miss! . . . Oh, finally. There you are.
HELEN. What is it?
MRS. SPILLER. Oh, my—nnngg—it's your sister—*(whispers something in Helen's ear)*—Nnngg—
HELEN. My brother-in-law gave specific orders to send for the doctor at the first sign of anything.
MRS. SPILLER. Oh, but Miss Helen—nnngg—she says she doesn't want—nnngg—doesn't want a doctor at all—nnngg. Doctors—oh, you know about these doctors—nnngg. With God's gracious help . . .

Miele comes from the house.

HELEN. Miele! Go get Dr. Schimmelpfennig immediately!
MRS. SPILLER. But, Miss . . .

MRS. KRAUSE. *(From the window, dictatorially.)* Miele! You get y'rself up here!
HELEN. *(Imperiously.)* Miele, you will go for the doctor! *(Miele withdraws into the house.)* Well, then I'll have to go myself. *(She goes into the house and comes back out at once carrying her straw hat.)*
MRS. SPILLER. It'll—nnngg—go sour. If you go get the doctor, Miss Helen, it'll—nnngg—go sour for sure.

Helen walks right by her. Shaking her head, Mrs. Spiller returns to the house. As Helen turns into the pathway, upstage L., Kahl is seen standing behind his fence.

KAHL. *(Calls to Helen.)* What's goin' on over at your place? *(Helen does not pause, nor does she find it worth her while even to notice Kahl, let alone answer him. Kahl, laughing.)* Wh-wh-at are y'gonna do—b-butcher an ol' sow today?

Act V

The set as in Act I. Time: around 2:00 A.M. The room is in total darkness, pierced only by a shaft of light shining through the open middle door from the illuminated hallway. The wooden stairway leading to the upper floor is also clearly lit. The dialogue in this act—with very few exceptions—is spoken in subdued tones.

Edward, carrying a light, enters through the middle door. He lights the gas lamp hanging over the dining table as Loth also enters by the middle door. [Brought along from Berlin by Hoffmann, Edward speaks the caustic working-class argot of the city.]

EDWARD. With all that's goin' on, it's gotta be humanly impossible to shut an eye around here, that's f'r sure.
LOTH. I didn't even *want* to sleep. I've been writing.
EDWARD. 'Zat a fact?! *(The lamp is finally lit.)* There! . . . Well, anyway, it sure is hard enough to. . . . Would y'like t'have pen 'n' ink, Doctor?
LOTH. When you've finished . . . if you'd be so kind, sir.
EDWARD. *(While placing pen and ink on the the table.)* If you're int'rested in my opinion, anybody who's a halfway honest man 'sgotta work 'imself to the bone f'r every lousy penny 'e gets. Can't even get a decent night's sleep. *(With increasing confidentiality.)* But this here outfit! They do absolutely nothin' at all. Laziest, good-f'r-nothin' bunch y'ever— . . . I'll bet you've gotta slave away day 'n' night just t'make a livin', Doctor—like all honest folks.
LOTH. Wish I didn't have to!
EDWARD. Me too! Or d'ya think I don't?
LOTH. I guess Miss Helen is with her sister?
EDWARD. Tell you the truth: she's a good girl. Doesn't leave her bedside f'r a moment.
LOTH. *(Checking his watch.)* Labor pains began at eleven this morning, which means they've already lasted fifteen hours—fifteen long hours!
EDWARD. God knows!—And that's what they call "the weaker sex." But she's really gaspin' f'r breath.

LOTH. Is Mr. Hoffmann upstairs, too?
EDWARD. Yeah—and let me tell ya, he's carryin' on jus' like a woman.
LOTH. I'm sure it's no small matter to have to sit there and watch.
EDWARD. You can say that again! Well, anyway, Dr. Schimmelpfennig just came. Now *there's* a man, let me tell ya: gruff as a drill sergeant, but inside—pure mush.... Hey, tell me, will ya, what ever happened to ol' Berlin since ... *(He interrupts himself with a)* Christ almighty! *(as Hoffmann and the doctor can be seen coming down the stairs.)*

Hoffmann and Schimmelpfennig enter.

HOFFMANN. You'll stay here now, won't you?
SCHIMMELPFENNIG. Yes. Now I'll stay.
HOFFMANN. That'll be good for me. Calm me down.—How about some wine? You'll have a glass of wine, won't you, Doctor?
SCHIMMELPFENNIG. If you really want to do something for me, let me have a cup of coffee instead.
HOFFMANN. Gladly.—Edward! Coffee for the doctor! *(Edward exits.)* You're ... are you satisfied with the way things are going?
SCHIMMELPFENNIG. As long as your wife's strength holds up, she isn't in any immediate danger. By the way, why didn't you call in the young midwife? As I recall, I recommended her to you.
HOFFMANN. My beloved mother-in-law!... What can I do? To be perfectly honest, my wife doesn't have any confidence in the young woman either.
SCHIMMELPFENNIG. But your ladies place complete confidence in that fossilized hag?! Lots of luck!—You want to go back upstairs?
HOFFMANN. Tell you the truth: I'm sort of uneasy down here.
SCHIMMELPFENNIG. It would be better, of course, if you went someplace else altogether—out of the house.
HOFFMANN. Even if I tried, I'd only... Loth! You're still here, too! *(Loth rises from the sofa in the darkened downstage R. area and walks over toward the two men.)*
SCHIMMELPFENNIG. *(Completely surprised.)* Well, I'll be damned!
LOTH. I'd heard that you were here. I was going to track you down tomorrow without fail. *(They shake hands enthusiastically. Hoffmann takes advantage of the moment by going over to the buffet and quickly slugging down a glass of cognac before he tiptoes out of the room and creeps back up the wooden stairs.)*

At first, the conversation between the two old friends is unmistakably colored by a certain quiet restraint.

SCHIMMELPFENNIG. So—it seems you've decided to forget that—hahaha—ridiculous old business? *(He puts down his hat and cane.)*
LOTH. Long ago, Schimmel!
SCHIMMELPFENNIG. Well, so have I, as you can imagine. *(They shake hands again.)* There've been so few pleasant surprises in this godforsaken hole of a town that it feels absolutely queer to stumble onto this one. Strange, running into each other here, of all places. Really strange!
LOTH. You dropped clear out of sight, Schimmel. Otherwise I'd have tried to dig you up long ago.
SCHIMMELPFENNIG. I just did a quick dive, like a seal. Decided to do a little deep-sea research. In about a year-and-a-half I hope to surface again. You have to be financially independent, you know, if you're going to do anything useful.
LOTH. So, you're raking it in here, too?
SCHIMMELPFENNIG. Of course, and as much as possible, for that matter. What else is there to do around here?
LOTH. You might at least have let someone hear from you.
SCHIMMELPFENNIG. If you'll excuse me, had you heard from me, I, in turn, would have heard from all of you—and I most emphatically wanted to hear nothing. Nothing—nothing at all. That would simply have gotten in my way while I was busy panning for gold.

Both men pace slowly up and down the room.

LOTH. Well, then you shouldn't be too surprised to learn that every one of them, to a man, wrote you off as a lost cause.
SCHIMMELPFENNIG. Just like them!—Bunch of bums!—I'll show 'em yet!
LOTH. Same old Schimmel—out of his corner and swinging!
SCHIMMELPFENNIG. Why don't *you* try living around these peasants for six years? Bunch of bastards—every one of them.
LOTH. I can imagine.—But how'd you ever manage to end up in Witzdorf?
SCHIMMELPFENNIG. It just happened. If you remember, I had to make myself scarce in Jena.[15]
LOTH. Was that before things caved in for me?
SCHIMMELPFENNIG. Sure. Short time after we'd quit living together. So, I went to Zurich and decided to take up doctoring. At first, to

---

15. A city of moderate size in Thuringia, now in the German Democratic Republic (East Germany), Jena was known as a seat of learning and scientific research. It was also the site of an important siege in the Napoleonic Wars.

have something to fall back on, just in case; but then it actually began to interest me. And today, I've got both body and soul invested in medicine.

LOTH. What about this town? How'd you get here?

SCHIMMELPFENNIG. Just like that! Very simple! After I got my degree, I said to myself: first things first, and first of all on the agenda was the accumulation of a large and neatly stacked pile of liquid assets. I thought: maybe America—South or North, maybe Africa, maybe Australia, maybe even the East Indies. Finally, it occurred to me that in the meantime my one little youthful indiscretion had either been long forgotten or had, at least, been outlived by the statute of limitations. So, I made up my mind to creep back and try my luck on the old turf.

LOTH. What about your Swiss medical exams?

SCHIMMELPFENNIG. I simply had to go through the whole song and dance all over again.

LOTH. Had to pass the state boards twice over?! Wheew!

SCHIMMELPFENNIG. Sure. Finally, I had the great good fortune to discover this fertile little patch of pastureland.

LOTH. You're hard as nails—enviably so.

SCHIMMELPFENNIG. As long as you don't collapse all of a sudden—but even that wouldn't be the end of the world.

LOTH. Do you have a large practice?

SCHIMMELPFENNIG. And how! Once in a while I don't get to bed till five in the morning—and then regular office hours begin again at seven.

Edward enters, bringing coffee.

SCHIMMELPFENNIG. *(Sitting down at the table, to Edward.)* Thank you, Edward. *(Then to Loth.)* I guzzle coffee—incredible quantities.

LOTH. You'd be better off to give that up.

SCHIMMELPFENNIG. What do you expect me to do? *(He takes little swallows.)* Well, as I told you—one more year—then all this screeches to a halt. . . . At least, I hope so.

LOTH. Don't you intend to practice at all anymore?

SCHIMMELPFENNIG. Don't think so. No—definitely no more. *(Pushes back the tray with the coffee dishes; wipes his mouth.)* By the way, let's see your hand. *(Loth holds out both hands toward him.)* Still unattached, hunh? Haven't dragged one home to your cave yet. Haven't found one, right? Not the species you were always hunting, anyway: basic earth mother, primitively vigorous, prime

Act V

breeding stock. Not that you're wrong. I mean, if you're going to do something, do it right or not at all. Or have you allowed your standards to slip a little on that issue?

LOTH. Not one bit. They are as rigorous as ever.

SCHIMMELPFENNIG. I wish the farmers around here shared your ideas. Slim chance of that, let me tell you. Degenerates—all the way down the line. *(He has taken his cigar case halfway out of his breast pocket but lets it slide back as he rises after hearing a sound from behind the partially closed door to the hallway.)* Wait a minute! *(He tiptoes to the door and listens. In the few moments between the sounds of the opening and closing of a door upstairs, we distinctly hear the moaning of the woman in labor. The doctor, turning to Loth, says softly)* Excuse me! *(and goes out.)*

For several seconds, while we hear doors slamming and people running up and down the stairs, Loth paces the room from end to end. Then he sits down in the easy chair, downstage L. Helen slips hurriedly through the door and throws her arms around Loth, who has not seen her coming from behind.

LOTH. *(Looking around, then also embracing her.)* Nellie! *(He draws her down, and despite meeting mild resistance, manages to sit her on his knee. Helen cries while he kisses her.)* Don't cry, Nellie! Why all these tears?

HELEN. Why? Oh, I don't really know! . . . I keep thinking—that you won't be here. I felt so frightened just a short while ago. . . .

LOTH. How come?

HELEN. Because I heard you walk out of your room.—And then there's my sister.—Oh, pity us poor women!—She's been suffering so much.

LOTH. That kind of pain is soon forgotten, and it's not as if she were in danger of dying.

HELEN. But she *wants* to die. . . . She keeps moaning: "Let me die; just let me die!" . . . It's the doctor! *(She jumps up and rushes into the conservatory.)*

SCHIMMELPFENNIG. *(While entering.)* Now I really do wish that the little woman upstairs would hurry up a bit! *(He sits down next to the table, takes out his cigar case once again, pulls out a cigar, and lays it down.)* You'll come with me to my place afterwards, right? I've got one of those contraptions hitched to a pair of old plugs outside. It ought to get us where we're going. *(Tamping his cigar against the edge of the table.)* Ah, yes—married bliss! Nothing like it! . . . Chee-rist! *(Striking a match.)* So—you're still footloose and fancy free! Happy, healthy, and very single, right!

LOTH. You might have waited a few more days before asking me that.
SCHIMMELPFENNIG. *(Whose cigar is finally lit.)* Hunh? . . . Ohoooo! I see! *(Laughing.)* So, you've finally come over to *my* side.
LOTH. Are you still so terribly pessimistic about women?
SCHIMMELPFENNIG. Terribly?? Incredibly!! *(Watching the smoke rise from his cigar.)* I used to be a pessimist by instinct—now I'm a pessimist on principle.
LOTH. As a result of hard experience, no doubt?
SCHIMMELPFENNIG. And how! My shingle reads: Obstetrics and Gynecology! Believe me, I prescribe the practice of medicine as a magnificent font of wisdom—not to mention sanity. It is particularly effective in the treatment of all manner of delusions.
LOTH. *(Laughs.)* Well, it seems we shouldn't have much trouble falling into our old manner of discourse. . . . Actually, I ought to let you know that I haven't come over to your side at all. Now less than ever! . . . So, you've changed hobbyhorses in midstream, have you?
SCHIMMELPFENNIG. Hobbyhorses?
LOTH. Well, the role of women in society was, so to speak, your pet subject back in the old days, wasn't it?
SCHIMMELPFENNIG. Oh, I see! What makes you think I've traded it in?
LOTH. Well, if you have an even lower opinion of women today than . . .
SCHIMMELPFENNIG. *(Somewhat provoked, he gets up and walks back and forth while speaking.)* I don't have a low opinion of women.—Not by a long shot!—I only have a low opinion of marriage . . . of marriage and, if there's anything else of which I have a low opinion, of men! You think the problem of women in society doesn't interest me any more? What do you think I've been doing here for six years, slaving away like a brewery horse? Only for this: so that someday I shall be able to devote all the available powers within me to the solution of that problem. Haven't you known that from the very beginning?
LOTH. How on earth should I have known?
SCHIMMELPFENNIG. Well, as I told you . . . I've already gathered a considerable body of significant evidence that is going to be extremely useful. . . . Shhh! . . . You know, I've developed this dreadful habit of yelling. *(He becomes quiet, perks up his ears, goes to the door to listen, and returns.)* So, tell me, what brings *you* to the land of the plutocratic peasants?
LOTH. I'd like to investigate the social conditions around here.
SCHIMMELPFENNIG. *(In a subdued voice.)* Not a bad idea! *(Still more softly.)* I can provide you with a healthy amount of evidence, too.

Act V

LOTH. I'm sure you can. After all, you must be thoroughly conversant with local affairs. For instance, what does the pattern of family life look like?

SCHIMMELPFENNIG. Universally grim! . . . Drunkenness, gluttony, inbreeding and all points west. Result: degeneration—all the way down the line.

LOTH. With exceptions, of course.

SCHIMMELPFENNIG. Hardly any!

LOTH. *(Troubled.)* Weren't you ever tempted to . . . to marry one of the golden daughters of Witzdorf?

SCHIMMELPFENNIG. *(A sound of violent disgust is followed by.)* Man, what do you take me for? You could just as well ask me whether I have a strong enough stomach to . . .

LOTH. *(Very pale.)* Wh-why?

SCHIMMELPFENNIG. Because . . . Something wrong with you? *(He stares at Loth for several seconds.)*

LOTH. Not a thing! What should be wrong with me?

SCHIMMELPFENNIG. *(Suddenly very pensive, he takes a few steps, stops sharply, gives a slow, soft whistle, takes a fleeting glance at Loth, and then mutters to himself.)* That's bad!

LOTH. Why this strange reaction all of a sudden?

SCHIMMELPFENNIG. Shhh! *(He listens for a sound from upstairs, then quickly leaves the room by the middle door.)*

HELEN. *(After several moments enters through the middle door and calls.)* Alfred!—Alfred! . . . Oh, you're here, thank God!

LOTH. Well, did you expect me to have run away?

They embrace.

HELEN. *(Pulls back. With unmistakable terror in her face and voice.)* Alfred!

LOTH. What is it, darling?

HELEN. Nothing, nothing!

LOTH. But there's clearly *something*!

HELEN. You just seemed so . . . so cold, so distant. . . . Oh, I imagine the most unbelievably stupid things.

LOTH. What's the situation upstairs?

HELEN. The doctor's arguing with the midwife.

LOTH. Isn't it just about over by now?

HELEN. How should I know? But when . . . when it *is*, I think we . . .

LOTH. What? . . . What are you trying to say? Will you please tell me?

HELEN. When it's over, we ought to leave here. Right away! Immediately!

LOTH. If you really think that's the best way, Nellie—

HELEN. Yes! It is! Waiting's no good! This will be best—for you and for me. If you don't take me away from here soon, you never will. You'll just leave me in the lurch, and then . . . then . . . I'll be destroyed.

LOTH. Why can't you trust me at all, Nellie?

HELEN. Don't say that, darling. It's easy to trust you, anyone would have to trust you! . . . Once I'm really yours, then . . . you'll never leave me then, will you? *(As if beside herself.)* I beg you! Don't go away! Don't ever leave me! For God's sake, Alfred—don't ever go! It'd be all over for me. I'd die if you left here without me.

LOTH. You certainly are a strange creature! . . . And you still insist you trust me? . . . Or maybe it's just that they're harassing you here, tormenting you beyond endurance—more than I even dared . . . No matter what, we leave tonight. I'm ready. Anytime you wish, we can go.

HELEN. *(With a cry of almost jubilant gratitude, she throws her arms around his neck.)* Darling! *(She kisses him hysterically, then hurries out.)*

Dr. Schimmelpfennig comes in through the middle door in time to see Helen disappear into the conservatory.

SCHIMMELPFENNIG. Who was that?—Oh, yes! *(To himself.)* Poor thing! *(With a sigh, he sits down by the table, finds his old cigar, tosses it aside, takes a fresh one from his case and starts to tamp it against the side of the table, across which he gazes pensively.)*

LOTH. *(Watching him.)* That's exactly the way you used to smash your cigars before smoking them eight years ago.

SCHIMMELPFENNIG. Could be! *(As he has finished lighting it.)* Now, you listen to me!

LOTH. What do you want?

SCHIMMELPFENNIG. I take it for granted that as soon as all this business upstairs is done and over with, you're coming with me.

LOTH. Sorry to say, that's not possible.

SCHIMMELPFENNIG. You know, every once in a while, like everyone else, I get this urge to enunciate quite thoroughly everything that is weighing on my mind.

LOTH. Which I feel every bit as much as you do. But you must realize that it is absolutely beyond my power to go with you today.

SCHIMMELPFENNIG. What if I were to explain to you, most emphatically and with utmost solemnity, that this is a specific matter of the greatest importance that I want to—better yet, *have* to discuss with you, Loth? And tonight!!

LOTH. That's silly! You don't expect me to take that dead seriously, do

Act V

you? It's waited all these years, and now it can't wait one more day?—You know me; I'm not being evasive; I wouldn't play games with you.

SCHIMMELPFENNIG. So, there actually *is* some truth to it! *(He gets up and walks around.)*

LOTH. Some truth to what?

SCHIMMELPFENNIG. *(Standing still, face-to-face with Loth, he looks him straight in the eye.)* That there's something cooking between you and Helen Krause.

LOTH. Me and . . . ? Who said any—?

SCHIMMELPFENNIG. How could you manage to get entangled with anyone from this family?

LOTH. Man, where do you get your information?

SCHIMMELPFENNIG. It wasn't so very hard to guess.

LOTH. Well then, drop it, for God's sake, or I'll have to . . .

SCHIMMELPFENNIG. So, it seems you two are properly engaged.

LOTH. Call it what you will. In any case, we've come to an understanding.

SCHIMMELPFENNIG. That doesn't answer my question. How did you get involved with *this*, of all families?

LOTH. Hoffmann and I were friends in college. He was also a member—granted, a corresponding member—of my colonizing organization.

SCHIMMELPFENNIG. I heard about that little enterprise while I was in Zurich.—So, he used to hang around with *you*! That goes a long way toward explaining how he got to be such a pitiable hermaphrodite.

LOTH. He's a fence-straddler. No doubt about it.

SCHIMMELPFENNIG. Actually, he's even less than *that*.—But, man-to-man now, Loth, are you really serious about this? I mean this thing with the Krause girl?

LOTH. Well, of course, I am!—I committed myself! You're not going to question my integrity, are you?

SCHIMMELPFENNIG. All right! All right! Don't have a fit about it! . . . You know, it wouldn't have hurt you to change a little in all these years. Hell, no! A small sense of humor wouldn't exactly be a liability in your case! I can't see why you have to take everything so damn seriously.

LOTH. I take things more seriously than ever. *(He gets up and walks beside, but always a little behind, Schimmelpfennig.)* And there's no way you could know—and I couldn't even explain it to you—what this relationship means to me.

SCHIMMELPFENNIG. Hmnn!

LOTH. Man, you have no idea what it's like to feel like this. If you've never experienced it yourself, you don't know that it's like. And if you have, you know that the desire is enough to drive you insane.

SCHIMMELPFENNIG. The devil only knows what makes an allegedly rational man come by this mindless "desire."

LOTH. Don't consider yourself immune. It could even happen to you yet.

SCHIMMELPFENNIG. Fat chance!

LOTH. You sound like a blind man trying to describe color.

SCHIMMELPFENNIG. I wouldn't give you *that* for such a dose of temporary euphoria! Ridiculous! And temporary is what it is, you know. Marriage is permanent, a life sentence. . . . You're building on a foundation that makes sand look good.

LOTH. Euphoria! Euphoria, you call it! That only goes to show that you don't know what you're talking about. Sure, euphoria is temporary, and I've been known to have had attacks of it. Granted! But this is something entirely different.

SCHIMMELPFENNIG. Hmnn!

LOTH. I have approached this issue with clear and sober vision. I love her, but don't think that I—how shall I put this?—that I see her with . . . with all sorts of virtues and halos that aren't there. Not at all! She has faults, isn't even particularly beautiful. At least not—well, she isn't exactly homely either. Looking at her with total objectivity, I—well, actually it's entirely a matter of taste—I've never seen a prettier girl in my life. So, when you say "euphoria," I say "nonsense!" I am cold sober; my eyes are wide open. But, you see—and this is what is so remarkable—I can't conceive of myself without her any more. It's like . . . an alloy—that's how it seems to me, you know—like two metals so perfectly and intimately joined that it's impossible to say this is the one, and this is the other. It all seems so natural that it ought to be self-evident. In short—look, I may be babbling nonsense—or what may seem like nonsense to you—but this much is certain: if you can't understand this, you are a miserable, cold-blooded killjoy . . . a cynic, a wet blanket—just as *I* used to be—and *you* still are.

SCHIMMELPFENNIG. You've got it: the entire syndrome, down to the last symptom! Why is it that your sort is always up to the ears emotionally in the very things you have rejected intellectually? For instance, you and marriage. For as long as I've known you, you have been afflicted with this disastrous mania for getting married.

LOTH. It's instinct with me—sheer instinct. God only knows, I fight it as best I can, but it's hopeless.

Act V

SCHIMMELPFENNIG. When you get right down to it, a man can overpower even an instinct.
LOTH. Certainly, if there's any purpose in doing so. If it makes sense.
SCHIMMELPFENNIG. Is there any sense in getting married?
LOTH. There is indeed. Now you're talking about something that has purpose! At least for me. You have no idea how I've been barely scraping by till now. I don't want to get sentimental, but maybe I didn't feel it so keenly either. Maybe I wasn't as fully aware as I am now that all my endeavors and aspirations had made me empty, almost machinelike. No soul, no fire, no life! Who knows if I even really believed in anything any more? But as of today, that's all poured back into me. I feel so fantastically full—complete, spontaneous, happy! . . . Oh, what's the use? You wouldn't understand anyway.
SCHIMMELPFENNIG. The things your type needs to keep his head above water! Faith, love, hope! As far as I'm concerned, that's all a bunch of garbage. The fact of the matter is simply this: the human race is croaking, and the best we can do is to make its final agony as bearable as possible with the help of narcotics.
LOTH. Your latest stance on the subject?
SCHIMMELPFENNIG. Already five or six years old—and not likely to change.
LOTH. Congratulations!
SCHIMMELPFENNIG. Thanks!

A long pause.

SCHIMMELPFENNIG. *(After several uneasy attempts to begin.)* Look . . . unfortunately, this is the way it is: I feel that it is my responsibility . . . I absolutely owe you an explanation. I believe that you will not be able to marry Helen Krause.
LOTH. *(Coldly.)* Oh, is that your considered opinion?
SCHIMMELPFENNIG. Yes, that's my opinion. There are obstacles present, which, for you in particular . . .
LOTH. Listen! Don't, for God's sake, have any scruples on that account. The situation isn't nearly as complicated as all that. As a matter of fact, it's actually dreadfully simple.
SCHIMMELPFENNIG. "Simply *dreadful*" is more like it.
LOTH. I mean as far as the obstacles are concerned.
SCHIMMELPFENNIG. So do I—at least in part. But I'm talking about the rest of it, too. I just can't believe that you know the conditions here for what they really are.

LOTH. I do, however, know them quite precisely.
SCHIMMELPFENNIG. Then it must necessarily follow that you have drastically revised your basic principles.
LOTH. You'll have to express yourself a bit more clearly, if you don't mind, Schimmel.
SCHIMMELPFENNIG. You must unquestionably have dropped your primary requirement regarding marriage, although you did clearly hint that you placed as much importance as ever on the breeding of offspring sound in mind and body.
LOTH. Dropped it? What makes you think that I . . .
SCHIMMELPFENNIG. Then there's nothing that I can conclude other than . . . that you really *don't* know the circumstances. You do not know, for example, that Hoffmann had a son who, at the age of three, was destroyed by alcoholism.
LOTH. Wha . . . what are you saying?
SCHIMMELPFENNIG. I'm sorry, but I've got to tell you. After that, you can still do whatever you please. The affair wasn't exactly a pleasure, believe me. They were visiting here, just as they are now. They called me—half an hour too late. The child had bled to death long before I got there. *(Loth, showing visible signs of profound shock, hangs on the doctor's every word.)* The silly little tyke had reached up and grabbed the vinegar bottle, thinking his beloved rotgut was in it. Bang went the bottle, and the child fell right onto the broken glass. . . . Down here, you see, that's the saphenous vein. It was completely severed.
LOTH. Wh . . . whose child, did you say?
SCHIMMELPFENNIG. Hoffmann's and hers—the same woman who is up there once again to . . . and she drinks too, drinks herself into endless stupors, drinks whatever she can get her hands on.
LOTH. Then it . . . it isn't from Hoffmann that it's inherited.
SCHIMMELPFENNIG. By no means! The man suffers tragically under this curse, as much as he is able to suffer at all. Of course, he knew he was marrying into a family of sots. The old man spends his entire life draped over the bar.
LOTH. Of course—that's it.—I begin to understand a number of things.—No! I understand it all—everything! *(After a heavy silence.)* That means that her life here . . . Helen's life . . . it's . . . it's a—how shall I say it? There aren't any words for it. It's . . .
SCHIMMELPFENNIG. Try calling it what it *is*: horrible! Believe me, I know . . . I understand. I also understand, and did from the start, how you could get stuck on her, but as I've been trying to tell you . . .
LOTH. All right! Enough!—I get the point! . . . Isn't there . . . couldn't

we convince Hoffmann to . . . do something? Maybe *you* could convince him. She's got to be taken away from this cesspool.
SCHIMMELPFENNIG. Hoffmann?
LOTH. Yes. Of course, Hoffmann.
SCHIMMELPFENNIG. You don't know him very well, do you? . . . I don't think he's actually corrupted *her* yet, but I'm sure he's already corrupted her reputation.
LOTH. *(In a rage.)* If he has, I'll kill him! . . . Do you really believe . . . I mean, do you really think Hoffmann capable of . . .
SCHIMMELPFENNIG. Of *anything*! I think him capable of anything that might contribute even slightly to his own gratification.
LOTH. But she's—the purest creature on the face of the earth. *(Slowly, Loth picks up his hat and cane and puts on his shoulder bag.)*
SCHIMMELPFENNIG. What do you plan to do, Loth?
LOTH. I . . . I can't see her . . . again!
SCHIMMELPFENNIG. So, you've come to a decision?
LOTH. To do what?
SCHIMMELPFENNIG. To dissolve the relationship.
LOTH. What other decision can I make?
SCHIMMELPFENNIG. As a physician, I can tell you that there are known cases in which such inherited ills have been suppressed. And you, of course, would certainly provide your children with a rational upbringing.
LOTH. Some such cases may occur.
SCHIMMELPFENNIG. And the probability is not all that minimal that . . .
LOTH. That sort of thing is of no help at all, Schimmel. This is the way it is: there are three possibilities. Either I marry her, and then . . . No, that's a way out that simply doesn't exist. Or—the traditional bullet. At least a man could finally put an end to his troubles. But that's an extreme we haven't reached yet, a luxury we can't afford at present. Which leaves number three—Live! Fight! More and harder! Keep on fighting! *(His glance falls on the table where he notices the writing materials that Edward has brought. Loth sits down, takes pen in hand, hesitates, and says.)* Maybe it would still be better to . . .
SCHIMMELPFENNIG. I promise you that I'll explain the circumstances to her as clearly as possible.
LOTH. I know, I know! It's just that . . . there's nothing else I can do. *(He writes, puts the note in an envelope, and addresses it. He gets up and shakes hands with Schimmelpfennig.)* For whatever's left to be done—I'm depending on you.
SCHIMMELPFENNIG. You'll come to my place, right? My coachman will drive you over.

LOTH. Look, Schimmel . . . shouldn't we at least *try* to get her out of this . . . this man's clutches? . . . If things go on as they are, she's bound to fall prey to his selfish manipulations.
SCHIMMELPFENNIG. You're a good man, old friend of mine, and I'm really sorry for you, but will you let me give you a small piece of advice? Don't rob her of what . . . what very little you're leaving her with.
LOTH. *(After a deep sigh.)* This, too, shall pass. . . . Maybe, you're right.—As a matter of fact, I know you are.

We hear footsteps coming quickly down the stairs. In the next instant, Hoffmann rushes in.

HOFFMANN. Doctor, please, for God's sake . . . she's unconscious . . . the contractions have stopped. . . . Don't you think it's about time you . . .
SCHIMMELPFENNIG. I'm coming up. *(To Loth, meaningfully.)* Good-bye! *(To Hoffmann, who starts to follow him.)* Mr. Hoffmann, I must ask you to . . . any interference or disturbance could be disastrous . . . I'd much prefer you to stay downstairs.
HOFFMANN. You're asking a lot, but . . . whatever you think.
SCHIMMELPFENNIG. It's only what's best. *(Exits while Hoffmann remains.)*
HOFFMANN. *(Noticing Loth.)* I'm so worked up, I'm shaking all over. . . . Say, are you leaving?
LOTH. Yes.
HOFFMANN. Now, in the middle of the night?
LOTH. I'm only going as far as Schimmelpfennig's.
HOFFMANN. Oh, yes. That's right. Well . . . with the turn of events here, staying with us isn't much of a pleasure any more. . . . Well, then . . . Good luck! I wish you the very . . .
LOTH. Thank you for your hospitality.
HOFFMANN. And how about that project of yours? What do you have in mind?
LOTH. What project?
HOFFMANN. I mean your work, your research, that study you were planning to do on economics in our neck of the woods. I should tell . . . in fact, as a friend, I want to beg you with all my heart . . .
LOTH. You can stop worrying. By tomorrow, I will have left this place far behind me.
HOFFMANN. That's really—*(Interrupts himself.)*
LOTH. "Nice of you." Is that what you were about to say?
HOFFMANN. Well, not really—that is, yes—in a way, it is. Anyway

you'll have to excuse me now; I'm so terribly upset. Don't forget, you can always count on me! Old friends are still the best friends. Good-bye. 'Bye now. *(Exits through the middle door.)*
LOTH. *(Before walking out the door, he turns around once more and takes a long look around the entire room as if to burn it into his memory. Then to himself.)* Well—I might as well go now. *(One last look, and he leaves.)*

The room remains empty for a few moments. We hear muffled voices and the sound of footsteps. Then Hoffmann appears. As soon as he has closed the door behind him, he takes out his little notebook and goes over some figures with strikingly disproportionate equanimity. He stops, listens, becomes restless, strides over to the door, and listens again. Suddenly, someone runs down the stairs, and Helen bursts in.

HELEN. *(While still outside.)* Brother! *(While coming through the door.)* Brother!
HOFFMANN. What's wrong?!
HELEN. Steel yourself: stillborn!
HOFFMANN. Oh my God! *(He rushes out.)*

Helen is alone. She looks around and calls softly: Alfred! . . . Alfred! *Receiving no answer, she calls again, this time in rapid succession:* Alfred! Alfred! *She hurries to the door of the conservatory and peers in. Then she goes into the conservatory, but reappears shortly:* Alfred! *Her anxiety mounting, she cranes her neck to look out the window, downstage L.:* Alfred! *She opens the window and climbs up on a chair standing in front of it. At this very moment, a shriek resounds from the yard. It is the braying of her drunken father; the old farmer is making his way home from the inn:* Whooooo-haaaa! Hey! Ain't I a gor-geoush hunk o' man? An' ain't I got a gor-geoush wife? . . . An' ain't I got a couple o' gor-geoush daughtersh, hey? . . . Whoo-heeeee! *A short cry escapes Helen's lips, and she runs toward the middle door like a hunted animal. From there, she discovers the letter which Loth has left lying on the table. She runs to it, tears it open, and skims it while audibly blurting out several of its salient words:* "Insurmountable!" . . . "Never, ever again!" *She drops the letter and staggers slightly:* It's over! *She pulls herself together, holds the sides of her head with her hands, and cries out sharply and desperately:* It's all over! *She rushes out through the middle door. From outside we hear Krause's voice, already much nearer:* Heeee-whooooo! Ain't thish farm all mine? An' ain't I got a gor-geoush wife? An' ain't I one gorgeoush man? Ha-ha-ha-heeeyy! *Helen, still on her half-crazed search for Loth, comes back in by way of the conservatory and meets Edward, who has come in to get something from Hoffmann's room. She accosts him:* Edward! *He answers:*

Yes, Miss Krause? *Whereupon she continues:* I want . . . want to . . . see Dr. Loth. . . . *Edward answers:* Dr. Loth has driven away in Dr. Schimmelpfennig's carriage. *He then disappears into Hoffmann's room.* It's true! *Helen cries, and for a moment keeps herself from collapsing only with great difficulty. Suddenly she is possessed by a frenzied energy. She runs downstage R. and seizes the hunting knife with its decorated sheath which hangs from the stag's antlers above the sofa. She conceals the knife and stays quietly in the dark shadows of the downstage area until Edward, emerging from Hoffmann's room, has exited through the middle door. Krause's voice, closer and clearer by the moment:* Whooo-heeee! Ain't I a gorgeoush hunk o' man? *Responding to this sound as to a signal, Helen darts decisively toward Hoffmann's room and disappears into it. The stage is empty, and we continue to hear the farmer's voice:* Heeeyy! Ain't I got th' bes' lookin' teeth y'ever saw, huuunh? . . . an' ain't I got a gor-geoush farm? *Miele enters by the middle door. She looks around searchingly and calls:* Miss Helen! *And once again:* Miss Helen! *While we hear Krause's rawly insistent:* Th' money'sh all mine! *By now, Miele, without further hesitation, has disappeared into Hoffmann's room, the door of which she leaves open. Within an instant, she charges back out, obviously shocked into hysteria. Screaming [and not knowing which way to turn], she spins around two or three times. Then, still screaming, she bolts out the middle door. Her uninterrupted howling, less audible the further away she runs, is nevertheless heard for several seconds more. Finally, we hear the opening and clanging shut of the heavy front door, the noisy footsteps of the farmer as he stumbles around in the hall, and his rough, nasal, slobbering drunkard's voice which is now almost in the room through which it echoes:* Whooo-haaaa! . . . Ain't I got a couple o' gor-geoush daughtersh?!

Select Bibliography

English Translations of *Vor Sonnenaufgang*

Hauptmann, Gerhart. *Before Dawn*. Translated by Leonard Bloomfield. *Poet Lore* 20 (1909): 241–315.
———. *Before Dawn*. Translated by Ludwig Lewisohn. In *The Dramatic Works of Gerhart Hauptmann*, edited by Ludwig Lewisohn, vol. 1: 1–193. New York: B. W. Huebsch, 1912.
———. *Before Dawn*. Translated by Richard Newnham. In *Three German Plays*, pp. 43–140. Harmondsworth: Penguin Books, Penguin Plays (no. PL 46), 1963.
———. *Before Sunrise* [incomplete]. Translated by James Joyce. In Jill Thompson Perkins, *Joyce and Hauptmann: "Before Sunrise."* San Marino, Calif.: Huntington Library Publications, 1978.

Selective Secondary Bibliography of Recent Works in English

Bithell, Jethro. *Modern German Literature, 1880–1950*. 3rd ed. London: Methuen, 1959. (Originally published as *Modern German Literature, 1880–1938*. London: Methuen, 1939.)
Garten, Hugh F. *Gerhart Hauptmann*. Cambridge: Bowes and Bowes, 1954.
———. *Modern German Drama*. 2nd ed. London: Methuen, 1964.
Gray, Ronald. *The German Tradition in Literature, 1871–1945*. Cambridge: At the University Press, 1965.
Knight, K. G., and Norman, F., eds. *Hauptmann Centenary Lectures*. London: University of London Institute of Germanic Studies, 1964.
Osborne, John. *The Naturalist Drama in Germany*. Manchester: Manchester University Press, 1971.
Perkins, Jill Thompson. *Joyce and Hauptmann: "Before Sunrise."* San Marino, Calif.: Huntington Library Publications, 1978.
Reichart, Walter A. "Fifty Years of Hauptmann Study in America (1894–1944): A Bibliography." *Monatshefte* 37 (1945): 1–31. Updated as "Hauptmann Study in America: A Continuation Bibliography." *Monatshefte* 54 (1962): 297–310.
Shaw, Leroy R. *Witness of Deceit: Gerhart Hauptmann as Critic of Society*. University of California Publications in Modern Philology, no. 50. Berkeley: University of California Press, 1958.

www.ingramcontent.com/pod-product-compliance
Lightning Source LLC
Chambersburg PA
CBHW031321150426
43191CB00005B/281